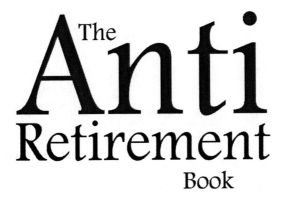

The Anti Retirement Book

By
Robert E. Levinson

© Copyright 2004 Robert E. Levinson. All rights reserved.

No part of this publication may be reproduced, stored in a retrieval system, or transmitted, in any form or by any means, electronic, mechanical, photocopying, recording, or otherwise, without the written prior permission of the author.

Printed in Victoria, Canada

National Library of Canada Cataloguing in Publication
Levinson, Robert E., 1925-
       The anti-retirement book / Robert E. Levinson.
ISBN 1-4120-1144-2
       I. Title.
HQ1062.L483 2004   646.7'9   C2003-904613-3

TRAFFORD

This book was published *on-demand* in cooperation with Trafford Publishing. On-demand publishing is a unique process and service of making a book available for retail sale to the public taking advantage of on-demand manufacturing and Internet marketing. **On-demand publishing** includes promotions, retail sales, manufacturing, order fulfilment, accounting and collecting royalties on behalf of the author.

Suite 6E, 2333 Government St., Victoria, B.C. V8T 4P4, CANADA

Phone	250-383-6864	Toll-free	1-888-232-4444 (Canada & US)
Fax	250-383-6804	E-mail	sales@trafford.com
Web site	www.trafford.com	TRAFFORD PUBLISHING IS A DIVISION OF TRAFFORD HOLDINGS LTD.
Trafford Catalogue #03-1523		www.trafford.com/robots/03-1523.html

10   9   8   7   6   5   4   3   2   1

To my wife Phyllis
for her love and devotion as my partner
for 55 years.

Thanks to Ray Dreyfack
who worked many hours to edit and
help coordinate the writing of this book.

A New Lease on Life

"The dictionary is the only place where success comes before work."'s
Anonymous

Are you inching towards the end of your job, worried about being downsized, or on the verge of selling your business? Are you employed at a job you hate, or working with a boss you don't like? Does your partner get on your nerves? Are you being overworked and underpaid?

Whatever your situation, if you are in your mid-40's or older it is neither too soon – nor too late – to DECIDE and PLAN how to spend the prime of your life.

In our lifetime we are faced by three major decisions:

1. What line of work will I choose as my career?
2. Who will I choose as my partner in marriage?
3. What will I do when my job or career is over – *or when I feel I'm ready for a new career?*

In my experience No. 3 is as important as any decision you ever made or will make in the future.

If you are a typical red-blooded American, your urge to succeed was probably a motivating drive of your life. Sensibly controlled, the struggle for success is what differentiates achievers from ordinary hacks. My personal definition of success is straightforward and simple:

- To **love** and be **loved**.
- To be **financially** stable.
- To be productively **active**.

vii

Lacking any one of the three makes life's satisfaction and fulfillment incomplete.

The wealthy person who doesn't know love is a failure. The man or woman, loved or not, financially stable or not, who leads an inactive boring life, is a flop.

Do you rate yourself a success or a failure?

What can this book do for you?

Decisions. Decisions. Decisions.

We are faced with decisions all of our lives. Minor decisions, major decisions; easy decisions, difficult decisions; decisions we can make on our own, and those with which we need help. Decisions that impact on our love life, social life, and careers.

While young and struggling to build a nest egg, meet child rearing and home maintenance commitments, fulfill obligations to the boss and customers, our hands were too often tied. We were forced to deal with decision constraints. We had to make decisions we preferred not to make because we had no other choice.

That was then. This is now. Today -- or soon -- with the kids grown, the boss and customers out of your hair, and other constraints no longer applicable, you are or will soon be, as President Jimmy Carter puts it, "free at last!". You're in a position to call the shots in a way that will be best for you. That's the good news.

The bad news is that millions of people in their mid-40's, 50's, and 60's – finally relieved of being forced to make lifestyle decisions – simply stop making them altogether. They don't plan for the future, or keep putting it off. In this way is spawned the much publicized couch or poolside potato. In this way millions of people, successful most of their lives, gradually convert into failures, bored, restless, and dissatisfied.

What will **THE ANTI-RETIREMENT BOOK** do for you? Hopefully, it will give you the psychological hotfoot so critically needed at this time of your life. Never has decision-making with

your future in mind been more important. This book presents a
Profitable and Productive Alternative and shows you how to make
it work in the most pleasant and painless way possible. It will help
you to answer the following questions and more:

- What are your deepest needs and desires?
- What are your true potential, your strengths and weaknesses?
- How can you cash in on your potent edge of know-how and experience?
- What lifestyle options are available?
- What are the pros and cons of launching a new career?
- How can you make financial and lifestyle plans compatible?
- How can you best evaluate your financial needs?
- Should you go into business for yourself, or take a job?
- Should you go into a family business?
- Should you take a partner?
- How can you most effectively and practically pay your social dues?
- Should you relocate and, if so, where?
- Should you seek professional counsel in making lifestyle decisions?
- Should you heed the advice of family and friends?
- How does your spouse fit into the picture?
- How can you develop a surefire lifestyle plan?

Most of all, **THE ANTI-RETIREMENT BOOK** will help you
re-**FIRE** instead of retire. It will show you **how to succeed *at the
ultimate career,* and at the time of your life when you can get the
most out of success!**

Robert E. Levinson
Boca Raton, Florida

Contents

Chapter 1
ANALYZE YOUR SITUATION
Soul-searching What You Want and Need   1

Chapter 2
TAKE A HARD LOOK AT YOUR OPTIONS
Creating a Life Plan   19

Chapter 3
MAP OUT YOUR FUTURE
Defining Your Strengths and Weaknesses   39

Chapter 4
EXPLORE EXCITING NEW POSSIBILITIES
Reviewing and Refining Your Life Plan   57

Chapter 5
FLOURISH AMIDST THE NEW REALITIES
Cash In On Your Edge   75

Chapter 6
SHOULD YOU RUN YOUR OWN SHOW?
Starting and Building a Business   91

Chapter 7
PRACTICE DOLLAR DIPLOMACY
Making Financial and Life Plans Compatible   109

Chapter 8
TAKE TIME FOR YOURSELF
Starting Now   127

Chapter 9
MAKE TIME FOR OTHERS
Giving Back for All You've Been Getting   145

Chapter 10
CALL YOUR OWN SHOTS
Showing People Who's In Charge   163

Chapter 1

Analyze your situation

Soul-searching What You Want and Need

Observe thyself as thy greatest enemy would do, so shalt thou be thy greatest friend.

Jeremy Taylor

Plato carried it a step further. "The unexamined life, " he said, "is not worth living."

Who are you? Want do you want? What do you need? Today? Tomorrow? Five, ten, fifteen years down the trail? Only you have the answer. Well intentioned friends, relatives, your spouse, kids, neighbors and coworkers may offer advice. But when you're lined up on the cue ball, it's your shot alone.

Sit down at the keyboard and make a list of your assets and liabilities. It's old advice but still in style and it will always be in style. Don't show the list to anyone, because if you are honest with yourself, self-disclosure can be embarrassing. There's no better way – or tougher way -- to find out who you really are than to *honestly* display your strengths and weaknesses in writing and, no less honestly, to analyze them.

That doesn't mean you can't, or shouldn't, seek help. But if you're not careful, misguided help could send you floundering in wrong directions. Don't let others impose their wills or mindsets on you. Feel you could use a bit of help and good counsel? Nothing wrong with that. But it is difficult to get true evaluation and guidance from friends, relatives, and others who are close to you and closely involved. There are too many distractions, too much self-interest, too many subjective personal needs and preferences which don't necessarily coincide with your own.

What you need are *objective* opinions. Baring your soul can be a humbling experience, especially to people who are important to you. Speak with your medical practitioner, ex-lawyer, ex-banker, ex-accountant, religious leader, someone devoid of self-interest whom you can confide in free from embarrassment and without holding back.

Think about it. You hold or held a responsible job, *you're* the one others came to for help or advice. That's why, with the tables turned, *objectivity* is critical. The one thing you don't need is confirmation that you're too old, over the proverbial hill, or in a down-sliding mode. Because there's no way you're too old – unless you tell yourself that you are.

Some images never desert you. I recall a discussion eight or nine years back with a friend and former associate, at the fifth tee if I remember correctly. Frank, recently retired, was a golfamaniac. Even now I can see him shaking his head. He couldn't see why, hitting on 60, I was still so actively engaged in so many enterprises and activities. "Why do you need it?" he asked. "You have more than enough to live on. It's time to retire, relax, take it easy."
'More than enough to live on'. He was talking about money, of course. But it takes more than money to live a life that is rich, full, and meaningful.

I ran into Frank a few months ago, now 65. He had given up golf years before and had turned into a poolside couch potato if there is such a thing, bored out of his skull. His story is by no means unusual. In my experience, the retirement world is overpopulated with "Franks". All the *early bird* boozers and schmoozers at his condo.

Cash In On Your Edge

Think about it. You are age 50, 55, 60, or that meaningless digit, 65. Take a cue from Ralph, not Frank. All his life Ralph did what he had to do to earn a living, advance on the job, fulfill his responsibilities to his family and employer. Unfortunately, what one *has* to do and what one *wants* to do don't always coincide. Forced into "retirement" at age 62, friends and even his wife Sue, urged, "Now's your chance to relax, take it easy, enjoy life."

Ralph smiled. "You mean vegetate, don't you?"

That wasn't Ralph's idea of enjoying life. His doctor asked, "What do you really *want* to do? Equally important, what are you *capable* of doing?"

Ralph's response served as a road map to the prime of his life.

Today, at 74, he is still going strong, doing what he always wanted to do, what he demonstrated during his career he was *able* to do: teach, write, lecture – not to mention tennis and biking. When friends say, "You're too old for that kind of stuff, Ralph replies, "Too old for what?"

Whatever your age, if you have years of experience and achievement behind you, you probably have at least one dominant "edge" along with an inventory of edges, some of which may be hidden. If you're a wiz at numbers or computer design, or have a talent for selling, therapy, machine repair, carpentry, fund raising, or anything else, that edge isn't going to curl up and die at age 60, 65, or any age.

More and more Americans -- and more and more American organizations -- are coming to this powerful realization. Eight out of 10 baby boomers, according to a poll by the American Association of Retired Persons – maybe AARP will consider changing its name to the American Association of Re-**FIRED** Persons -- plan to keep working at least part time after they retire. And an increasing number of recruiters are turning to this still largely untapped pool of workers in an effort to cash in on the vast amount of knowledge and experience therein.

Do you think 65 is "old"? If so, don't tangle with Milton Garland of Waynesboro, Pa., a mechanical engineer who, at age 102, still goes to the plant every day after 78 years at his job with the Frick Co. He puts in about 20 hours a week. An expert at what he does, interviewers try to determine the secret of his longevity. Does he have a special diet? Absolutely! "I eat everything but sauerkraut." On a more serious note, he gets the message across: The real secret of fruitful longevity, he believes, is living busily and productively from day to day every day.

How old is old? In *The Wall Street Journal* Clare Ansberry talks about "The Third Age". "Getting old is now characterized as a Third, or even Fourth, age. It is late adulthood, the second 50." Ansberry quotes Florence Klingsman, whose son is 50. He says he's getting old. "'Heck, Jackie,' says Mrs. Klingsman, 77, 'that's young. At 60 you're middle-aged'."

At what age should you quit? How old is too old? At age 73, Postmaster General Marvin Runyon, who already had three careers, said he wants at least two more. How old are you? At age 50, 55, or 60, do you think you've "had it"? Or are you ready for more?

Don't Sell Your Physical Prowess Short

How physically strong and able must you be to take on difficult and important work in your so-called "senior" years? Clearly, you must be in *reasonably* good health.? Too many people with minor ailments from arthritis to gastritis mentally undermine their health. Your heart, lungs, liver, brain, and other bodily components must function, not as if you're 30, but well enough to fuel your activity. The point to keep in mind is that age is not a bodily component.

Satchel Paige's thought provoker is worth repeating:

How old would you be if you didn't know how old you was?

It certainly is not the purpose of this book to underrate the importance of physical well-being. But a major purpose is to stress the importance and interconnection of *mental* well-being. They go hand in hand to ensure good physical health in general and continuing sexual prowess in particular. You can't have one without the other.

I've seen it time and again. I won't use his right name; it would embarrass him. But when Jim, age 59, an expert swimmer who excelled in tennis as well, was downsized from his job as a telephone utility man, his transformation occurred so rapidly it was shocking to family and friends. As a neighbor put it, "Almost overnight Jim seemed to age 20 years. He became haggard and pale, lost his zest for good food, complained about loss of sleep, lost interest in sex, worry frowns lined his forehead."

Finally, at his lusty wife's urging, he agreed to see a therapist. It took no more than a few sessions for his "edges" to start surfacing. "You may be right," the doctor conceded, "another job doing what you did for thirty years or more, might be hard to find. But what about your other skills? What about your knowledge and love of boats and refinishing furniture? What about your mechanical aptitude?"

It wasn't easy, but the message got through. Today Jim is employed in a boat yard working on repairs and refinishing. The job is harder and physically more demanding than what he did at the phone company. Is 59 too old to take on such a job? Jim's reply: "The exercise I get on this job keep me in better shape than ever." His earnings are about ten percent less, but he enjoys his work more than ever before. Jim is his old robust self again and he and Ann spend more time in the bedroom.

All In the Mindset

How old is too old for important and responsible work? Remember George McGovern? Even wonder what he's doing these days? At age 75, the longtime senator, historian, former innkeeper, and onetime presidential candidate, decamped to Rome with his wife Eleanor.

Vacation? Perhaps, except that in McGovern's lexicon vacation and vocation are synonymous. Is taking on the job of U.S. Ambassador to the U.N.'s Agency for Food and Agriculture too tough and demanding for a 75-year-old man. Senator McGovern doesn't think so. Asked when he planned to retire, he responded,

"I'll consider retirement when I get old."

Composer Burt Bacharach, pushing 73, was asked, "When will you stop?" He replied, "When I can get a standing ovation walking down the street in Santa Monica."

How old is too old for sexual gratification? A friend, 75, confided recently, "The best sex I ever had was from 50 to 70. I had total control, and I was smart enough to understand that good sex includes dimensions beyond the act itself. The worst sex I ever had was from 20 to 30. I'm not knocking it, but it wasn't complete." Bottom line: It is all in the mindset.

How *healthy* do you have to be to take on new challenges and opportunities? Controversial Mike Wallace of *Sixty Minutes* fame, in his eighties, has run a remarkable gamut of projects and jobs in his lifetime from reporter and correspondent to TV show superstar. In 1963 he turned down President Nixon's invitation to serve as his press secretary. He has taken on the tobacco industry and the military. Once hospitalized for severe depression, he currently wears a pacemaker that must be checked monthly. He is still going strong.

How healthy do you have to be? You don't have to juggle 80 pound weights. You have to be simply healthy enough to function normally.

Traditionally – a tradition I'm determined to help break if I can which is my motivation for writing this book – as many people grow older, 55, 60, or approaching the phony turning point of 65, their mindset tends to alter. Subconsciously, they view themselves as mentally, physically, even sexually, diminished.. They start to turn off the engine, sign up for a reservation in God's waiting room. *Especially if they have just been retired or downsized.* It could happen almost overnight as it did with Frank.

If you ever fought anything in your life, this is a mindset with which to do battle.

Rate Your Potential Realistically

President Jimmy Carter, on *Larry King Live* with Hugh Downs and Billy Graham, was asked by Larry, "What is the best thing about being old?" Carter's face crinkled into his appealing grin. "The complete freedom you have to make decisions about what you will do and how you will spend the rest of your life."

Freedom is great, but like your head it depends on how you use it. At certain junctures of our life crucial decisions have to be made. In one's 50s and 60s, the big challenge confronting us is: What's next? Where do I go from here?

Can you recall back to a time when you made a wrong major decision? How many of us cannot? Well, think back to that time. What was your mental condition? Your attitude? Your mindset? Were you time-pressured and under stress? Were you under someone's undue influence? Did your emotional involvement distort your good judgment?

I have seen it happen time again in my own experience and in the experience of others: Irrational decisions triggered by intrusive emotions. Or intrusive intruders. One of the advantages of being at or beyond life's "Second Stage" -- 50 or older -- is the common sense and maturity you can call on when decision time is at hand. A friend remarked recently, "I wish I understood my gifts, abilities, and potential as well at age 22 as I do now."

Kids are impulsive; they make rash judgments. "Adults" should know better. In my experience it makes sense in confronting career and life decisions to brainstorm them over a two or three week period, or longer than that if you feel the need. And if need be, with the guidance of an uninvolved person or two. This is by no means a plea for indecision stemming from lack of courage or fear which can be as damaging as impulsiveness. It's a plea for mature reflection. The idea is to put every major factor and consideration into play. Here again, a pencil and paper can be useful. Writing it down, item by item, helps you think about it.

What Are You Good At, and What Do You Like?

Combine these two questions into one, and you're on your way. Nine times out of 10, people enjoy what they are good at. Without enjoying an activity, it is hard to become good at it. But I've run into more than one situation where people were good at something they enjoyed, but a darned sight better at something else. In fact, there are some folks who excel at almost *everything* they tackle, because it is part of their nature to excel.

Amy excelled as a bookkeeper for a small office supply distributor. But she never stopped working on cars and one day reached the realization that this is what she really *wanted* to do. At age 58, she's not formally in business for herself. But the word got around in her small to mid-sized Connecticut town, and Amy's backyard is today the site of a moderately profitable enterprise.

Alice K -- Alice was for years a "giveaway artist". Friends, relatives, and coworkers in the office where she worked as a computer console operator, delighted in her talented sketches, water colors, and cartoons. An admiring uncle advised, "Alice, you shouldn't be working at a clerical job; you should be in business for yourself." She took his advice and at age 56 earns more money selling her work to individuals and local art dealers than she ever did at her job.

These examples speak for themselves. So many people fail to pinpoint their not-so-hidden abilities as rewarding career opportunities. As Alice's uncle observes, "All it takes is a little imagination and gumption."

Don't Let Your Kids Bug You

We love our children. We crow about their achievements. Their success and happiness multiplies our own feelings of joy and fulfillment. But as countless parents could confirm: "We love our kids, but we don't always love the way they love us."
Old notions persist. Kids, in most cases, are sincere. They're worried about us. Falling, fainting, making dumb decisions because

we're not as smart as they are. Mindlessly blowing our fortunes. They equate ages 60+ with vulnerability to all kinds of unknown disaster and trauma. They're more comfortable when they see us relaxing and "enjoying" life on a chaise by the pool. After all, how many people are hurt falling off chaise lounges.

My friend, Joseph M. was a Certified Public Accountant who advanced over the years to financial vice president of a major manufacturing company. Top rated as a professional in his industry – toys and novelties – he derived real pleasure from his job, from creating imaginative deals to solving complex dilemmas. But Joe's enjoyment of his vocation was second only to the kick he got from his avocation, developing computer software programs.

Joe's company was, and still is, old fashioned which is why he prefers I don't mention its name. Compulsory retirement at age 65. When wind blew through the industry that Joe was stepping down, offers for top financial jobs started filtering in by telephone, word of mouth, and executive recruiters. He thought about the offers, but not for long. He was too busy in his "home lab" designing specialized software programs he hadn't had time for when employed. Today at age 68 Joe puts in 30 to 40 hours a week in his lab. He does it partly for the fun and excitement he gets out of it, and partly for the income he derives from licensing his software to others.

When asked about his *main* motivation, he scratches his head. "I'm not sure; I like the money which is turning out to be more than I earned as a financial executive, but I think I enjoy the work even more, and the feeling of fulfillment I get when I come up with a can't-miss idea. Maybe what I like best of all, is the newness and freshness of my new life; on the old job I was beginning to feel burnout."

So, to repeat: What are you good at, and what do you like?

I have found that one of the best ways to learn about your abilities and work preferences is through involvement in community affairs. Better yet, by taking a leadership role in these activities. What if you never before functioned as a manager or supervisor? What if you never before had people working for you? All the more reason to give it a whirl. It doesn't have to be a big, important, heavily financed activity. It can be as modest as selecting and approving guest speakers at monthly meetings. Or checking the credentials of prospective member if that's a requirement. How, specifically, can you benefit from taking over a community project, acting as committee chair, for example, directing other members, and having them report to you?

1. **It's an antidote to timidity**. I have seen men and women develop almost overnight from shy, timid individuals afraid to air their views at a meeting, into self-assured and articulate people.

2. **You develop leadership abilities you never knew you were capable of.**

3. **You interact enjoyably and rewardingly with others.**

4. **You derive the satisfaction of giving of yourself and your time.**

5. **You make contacts that can stand you in good stead when it comes to deciding what you will do with your future.** In my own experience serving on boards and committees in community organizations in both Cincinnati and South Florida over the years, I couldn't begin to estimate the number of opportunity calls I received.

6. **Perhaps most important, you will develop friendships you will keep for the rest of your life.**

The Importance of Timing

The single most significant mistake I have observed made by people on the threshold of being either downsized or "retired" is their failure to plan in advance what they will do the next day, the next year, and the next decade or after.

I can think of no better example than my own. I don't want to beat the subject of my personal experience to death. But suffice it to say, I have had several careers during my lifetime, and in every single case dating back over the years, I had not been on the job for many weeks without planning, figuring out, and *preparing* for what my next job would be should I become fired, bored, or whatever.

My main function as a vice president at Lynn University is fund raising. The work I perform in this capacity, the skills and values I refined and developed, the friends and contacts I made, place me in an excellent position to move into another fund raising job, or some other line of work, should my job at Lynn fold tomorrow.

I have been in touch over the years with Don King, a key employee who worked for me at Steelcraft Manufacturing in Cincinnati a couple of decades ago. A talented manage and technologist, Don developed a hobby in his basement making picture frames for a variety of needs. He enjoyed the work immensely and got his wife interested at well., Thinking of the future, he encouraged his wife to open a small picture frame store in their neighborhood. The store filled a community need. The business grew and became increasingly successful. A few years ago Don left Steelcraft to join his wife running the store. A full time operation, for Don this represents a whole new career, planned and prepared for in advance. In addition to doing well financially, they are "having a ball" – trips, conventions, and a hobby turned into an enterprise. As Don puts it, "It's the way to stay young."

What *Else* Did You Do?

So many people fail to think about and cash in on talents and skills they relegate to the bottom drawer. Let me cite some examples of hidden talents turned into exciting and rewarding careers.

Harry B -- While employed as a production supervisor and with his children growing up, Harry spent years as a scoutmaster working with kids, and later on as a Little League coach. Opting for early rekindlement, he quit his job at age 57 and is happier and more relaxed today working full time at a neighborhood youth center.

Elaine B – An executive secretary for 32 years, Elaine devoted many hours of her spare time designing fancy and intricate embroideries for herself, family, and friends. Now re-**FIRED** at 62, she still works at the hobby she loves, but today it is more than a hobby. Working 20 to 30 hours per week, she sells her creations to local shops and, most recently to department store buyers.

Charley C – For years Charley, a former traffic expediter for a textile company, was the guy friends and neighbors came to when their TVs were on the blink. Today, re-**FIRED**, they still come to him at a store front that features a sign reading CHARLEY'S TV REPAIR.

Dino R – As a youngster, Dino helped his dad, a cabinetmaker, work at his trade. When his family emigrated to America Dino found a job with a Big Three Detroit auto maker, continuing cabinetry as a hobby. At age 53 he decided he enjoyed his hobby more than his job and turned it into a business. "Best move I ever made," says Dino who now has two men working for him.

Mary M – Mary also found a new lease on life thanks to her father who operated a three bay service station. "It always intrigued me watching Dad tackle and overcome complex and intricate problems." She not only watched, but learned. Dad passed on ten years ago and for over two decades Mary was employed

In its 65-year history, Julie Flaherty reports in *The New York Times*, Frederick Hartman, president of the Vita Needle Company in Needham, Mass., has never dismissed an employee. The concept of mandatory retirement is scoffed at. The average age at Vita Needles is 73. In fact, Mr. Hartman was "ticked off" when Mary Boyt, a key employee, decided to retire at age 89. "Her daughter pushed her into it," he says. "She was a great worker. I hope I'm as sharp at that age."

Rose Finnegan, a retired waitress, took a job at Vita Needle because her social security check wasn't enough to support her. Why Vita Needle? Replies Rose, "Who else is going to hire me at 86?" What motivates Mr. Hartman to be so gung ho about older employees? Good samaritanism? Not entirely. (Older workers) "are motivated;" he says, "they take care of the equipment; they don't have the P.T.A. meetings or the kids in day care. Most important, coming to work is a high priority."

In a nutshell, they're more loyal and dependable.

Perceptions vs. Realities

A nationwide survey conducted to help frame a national discussion about the future of Social Security in an aging society came up with some interesting and instructive revelations regarding perceptions of Americans aged 18-34 and the actual experience of Americans 65 and over.

Expectations and percentages:

	18-34 Perceptions	65 and Over Realities
MORE TRAVEL	77%	46%
MORE HOBBIES	76	56
LESS ACTIVE	69	41
NEW SKILLS	64	28
MORE RESPECT	62	53
LESS STRESS	58	50
SERIOUS ILLNESS	48	25
GET SOCIAL SECURITY	46	90
CAN'T DRIVE	47	15
GET MEDICARE	44	80
FEWER RESPONSIBILITIES	43	50
TROUBLE WALKING	41	30
LOSE BLADDER CONTROL	38	14
LESS SEX LIFE	32	37
BECOME SENILE	29	2
DEPENDENT ON KIDS	29	5
BE LONELY	26	24
BE POOR	13	18

A book could be written on each of these perceptions and realities. But a few are especially significant within the context of this book.

Conclusion No. 1 – With regard to health-related perceptions – less active, serious illness, can't drive, trouble walking, lose bladder control, become senile – it appears obvious that Americans over 65 *are not* as decrepit and over the hill as their kids perceive them to be.

Conclusion No. 2 – With regard to time-related perceptions – more travel, more hobbies, development of new skills -- one might conclude that too many seniors are *not* spending their time fruitfully and productive enough.

Conclusion No. 3 – With all the apparent *mis*conceptions in mind, seniors, not their kids, should be planning, preparing for, and deciding their futures, and they should be doing it **NOW** before their futures become their past.

Doing What's Best for Mom

What *is* best for Mom? I'll let you in on a secret. Only one person knows the answer to that question, and that person is Mom. Sometimes the kids think they know better than Mom what's best for her and more often than not they are wrong.

When Fairlawn, New Jersey's Elsie G was widowed, her daughter Rhoda lost no time urging her to come live with her in Oakland, California. "We have an extra bedroom and the kids will love it." The kids. All three of them, age 4, 6, and 8. Her son-in-law Bob echoed the plea. "Mom, we'd all love to have you." There was no question in Elsie's mind that she'd be welcome, but she had her doubts. She had scads of friends in Fairlawn, a rich social life, and she was on a whole bunch of committees, a dedicated community activist, not to mention her place in the choir. Money was no problem; she could afford to live anywhere. But she was in no mood to uproot her life at age 53, and relocate 3,000 miles away.

" Mom, We don't like you being alone."

'Alone'? Elsie thought, she was anything but alone. She had her friends and neighbors, rewarding work, and an apartment she loved. Rhoda was persuasive, but Elsie knew her own mind. She had no inclination to give up a life she enjoyed and become a built-in babysitter. So she thanked Rhoda and Bob and said, "No thanks. Hold that spare bedroom open for when I visit."

Her son Gerald who lives in Milwaukee told her, "Hey, Mom, don't let this get around, but that's the smartest decision you ever made."

Enough said. In most cases, seniors know instinctively and from experience what is best for them. If you're not sure, it can't hurt to seek advice from wise *objective* outsiders you respect. But not from well meaning family or friends.

Pluck Gems from Your Treasure Chest of Experience

The gems are there, but it's up to you to do the plucking. Take Elsie and her daughter's efforts to relocate her from New Jersey to California. A smart lady, she carefully considered her options, and in the process reviewed her experience. Her personal treasure chest contained not only activities from a lifetime of career, social, and community work, but her positive and negative recollections -- and *feelings* -- as well. Elsie loved her grandchildren and was a devoted young grandmother. Yet out of her lifelong memories she plucked a composite of all the times she had babysat the kids, her enjoyment and gratification short term, and how tiring it got when repeated for too long and too often. No, she had no intention of transforming from community activist to babysitter. All useful input when she made her decision.

The point is that your Treasure Chest is composed of a hodge-podge of feelings and reactions, plus and minus responses, mistakes and misjudgments, all of which are educational when crucial decisions have to be made.

15

It's Time To Take Inventory

Do you have a keyboard handy or – pardon the expression – a pencil and paper. Now is as good a time as any to look back over your lifetime starting from Phase One and Phase Two to the present. Your work experience, of course, is of prime importance, not only as employee but as social activist, hobbyist, community activist and volunteer.

Don't focus exclusively on your current job, and not necessarily on activities for which you were paid. Your challenge is to come up with the kind of involvement which, in the Third and Fourth Phase of your life, will result in maximum satisfaction and the kind of reward you will prize most.

What follows is a sampling of questions to review and evaluate in terms of your special talents and skills, likes and dislikes. Then rank your performance and contribution from the standpoint, first, of its value and usefulness to others, and then, with your personal preferences in mind.

- Of everything you have ever done, what in your opinion, is the one thing you are capable of doing best?

- Of everything you have ever done, what in your opinion, is the one thing from which you derived the most satisfaction and enjoyment?

- Of everything you have ever done, what more than anything else would you like to spend the next five, ten, or twenty years doing?

- How important – and how *necessary* – will financial income be to you and your family over the next five, ten, or twenty years? If the thing you would most like to do pays little or nothing at all, could you live with that?

- Is this one greatest preference of yours realistic? Are you capable of performance from a health standpoint? Have you explored "job" opportunities in this area, whether you regard it as employment or not?

- If you enjoyed your career as an employee, would you like to continue it as an entrepreneur? Do you have the needed resources to do it: Experience, financial, health, talent, etc.? Is there room in the marketplace for another business of this type? If you decide to go ahead with it, are you ready and willing to work your butt off, perhaps for years at the outset?

- Do you like where you live? How would you feel about relocating? How would your family feel about relocating?

- How does your family feel about all of the responses above?

This is no more than a sampling. How many questions can you add to this list with you and your family in mind? It is your personal inventory. It is your life. Plan ahead and it will flourish.

Chapter 2

Take a hard look at your options

Creating a Life Plan

"As a cure for worry, work is better than whiskey."
Thomas Edison

Anxieties -- financial, job, family, health -- have a way of dissipating when you take a good look at your options. One of the best options you have is the simplest option of all: Work.

When Peggy, widowed at age 48, learned that her inadequately insured daughter Ann's house had burned down, her immediate response was panic. She would chip in to help resettle Ann and her family, of course. But her own resources were also limited. The panic gradually faded to severe anxiety. That was no picnic either.

Her doctor gave her some good advice. "Get busy, and stay busy."

Talk about "silver linings" on dark ominous clouds. Recently downsized, and depressed because of it, the family misfortune was the best therapy Peggy could have obtained. She took her doctor's advice. Finding part time work was hard work and consumed most of her time. By the time she landed a job she was too busy to worry in earnest. She had done all she could. That's the best anybody can do. As Edison said, for Peggy work was a better cure for worry than whiskey or anything else. It helped her to ride out the storm.

But if you're a dyed in the wool hard core worrier, Edison's good

advice may not be enough to curb your anxiety. What other options are open? Here's a thought. If you're
going to worry, you might as well do it constructively. In this chapter I spell out what I mean.

Pinpoint Your Apprehensions

This advice isn't new. We all know that if you have a problem, step one toward a solution is to confront it openly and realistically. Let's apply this to the crucial subject at hand: **THE REST OF YOUR LIFE!** Face up to your anxieties as objectively as you can. Ask yourself: What, actually, are you worried about? Spell out the specifics. Spill them out on the table and deal with them one at a time. One by one ask yourself if it is worth losing sleep over? Equally important, does it adversely affect how you feel, what you do and how you do it, and the rightful course of your life?

Nothing makes better psychological or medical sense than to make this assessment. As any doctor will confirm, the impact of neurotic anxiety on one's physical and mental well-being can be devastating. Dr. Harold Michelson, a Paterson, New Jersey physician, once said, "If we could eliminate worry, the hospital population would be cut in half."

That's not to say all worries and concerns are to be brushed off as invalid. Task one is to determine which of your worries make sense, and which are futile. Task two is to get rid of the those that are needlessly plaguing you.
Task three is to take action to deal with those worries that make sense and which you can do something about.

One more time: What, actually, are you worried about? Let's look at some of the major concerns graying the hair of millions of working men and women in executive suites, middle management offices, and supervisory cubicles. In plants, offices, warehouses, retail, non-profit, and service jobs the world over.

Burnout and Boredom

Worry comes in a host of shapes, forms, and sizes.

Family worries: Are the kids doing alright? Is Bob's job in jeopardy? Is Susan's excessive fatigue serious? Can the wife's back trouble be cured? Job worries: Am I going to be downsized? Why does Ed get the choice assignments? Can I trust the boss to level with me? Money problems: Will we have to downgrade to a smaller house or apartment? Can we afford to keep financing the kids' college tuition? The list goes on and on.

Ethel was restless and edgy without knowing why. Her job as secretary to a sales executive had lost its former zest and excitement. Same thing over and over, day after day. Customer complaint letters and calls. Petty interdepartmental squabbles. Rush assignments that weren't really that urgent. Ethel used to enjoy coming to work but had begun to feel a gnawing anxiety. Had she taken the time to define why she felt that way, she might have been better able to understand that she was experiencing job burnout and why.

Burnout and boredom qualify as the nagging, slow creeping kind of job dissatisfaction. Yet they are among the most pernicious as Norman Mailer pointed when he stated that boredom slays more of existence than war.

Does worrying about burnout and boredom make sense? Maybe not. But it's understandable if you're stuck in a job that you hated for years and for one reason or another can do nothing about it. Even then, where is the percentage in worrying about a dilemma you can't change?

What makes more sense is to worry about a deadly work situation if there's something practical and realistic you can do to eliminate or alleviate it.

The dead end of being stuck in a job you don't like is a problem of mammoth proportions. If this crippling shoe fits it calls for deep objective analysis. Let's take a case in point to see how this can be done.

Harry's Dilemma

Harry Klein is an accountant employed by Pfizer Pharmaceutical Co. Fifteen years ago
when, employed by this company, the job was a challenge, exciting and fun.

A skilled professional employed by a good company, Harry advanced slowly from junior to senior status, received periodic increases in pay. He earns $67,500 and can't recall exactly when he knew he had reached a dead end, or faced the realization that he hated coming to work in the morning. Five years ago, six? No matter. In my experience, after eight or ten years, depressingly often, doing the same thing day after day with no new challenge or excitement, the job becomes a drag.

Does that leave Harry up the proverbial creek without a paddle? Maybe up the creek, but not without a paddle. The question, of course, is -- and this is always the
question -- what can Harry do about it? Let's review his circumstances.

HEALTH - Harry and his wife Ruth thankfully are both in reasonably good health.

FAMILY - The Kleins have always been a loving, close-knit family. But in recent months Harry's job stress and strain have been taking their toll.

FINANCIAL - The family is in relatively good shape financially with above-average holdings. But with one son a junior in college and another in graduate school, they are beginning to feel hard pressed.

STATE OF MIND - Harry's negative feeling about his job is having an adverse effect on his temperament. He is more often than in the past short tempered and irritable. He undergoes periods of depression, without being able to explain why to either Ruth or himself.

MARRIAGE - The Klein's marital relationship could not help but be adversely affected. A loving couple their relationship is starting to fray around the edges.

Harry's Action Plan

What can Harry Klein do in response to the boredom and burnout that is slowly undermining his temperament, personality, and marriage? What action options are open to him? Let's check them off one by one.

- He can do nothing. But settling for the status quo will clearly worsen the situation.

- Boring jobs rarely if ever automatically become less boring. Harry could throw up his hands in frustration, as is not uncommon, and quit, an ill advised and un planned decision considering his financial obligations.

- He could discuss the problem with his boss, usually a good idea. This might result in his being assigned new projects or a different kind of work that would make his job more interesting.

- He might seek a transfer to a different department or division of his company, which could enhance his lifestyle even if it reduces his income.

- A skilled and experienced professional, Harry could start checking the want ads, or touch base with friends and contacts. Even if he had to settle for a lower salary, he might be best advised to do so.

- With Harry's knowledge and experience he could go into business for himself, starting small if he's smart. Accountants do this every day.

- Harry's brother Frank runs a small but successful manufacturing company. He could accept the controller's job Frank has been urging him to take for months.

This is just a sampling of actions available to Harry in response to his obviously deteriorating lifestyle situation. The crucial question is <u>when</u> should such action be taken? The action itself could

23

take time -- weeks, months, even years, depending on which option appeals most to Harry, after discussing it with his wife Ruth. But a major point throughout this book is that the time to start planning for your future if you are fifty or older is now. Not tomorrow, today! Don't wait until it's too late. Especially if your present situation is distressing and worrisome.

Overcome Your Anxiety

My ten year old grandson steps up to the computer challenge with all the gusto he applies to a chocolate sundae heaped with whipped cream. Me? It scares the hell out of me. That's not to say everyone in their 50s, 60s, or 70s, finds the computer and other technology formidable. The Computer Club at Wynmoor, a retirement community in South Florida, is heavily attended by many retirees even more sophisticated than my grandson. Still, some of us, are intimidated by the infernal machine.

The problem takes on added complications when computer phobia holds one back on the job. The negative flip side of the electronic coin is that like it or not, the reality is that young people are less intimidated by the computer than their parents and grandparents in part because they are more recently involved with having to learn new skills. Had Bill Gates been in his 70's when he set out to conquer the world it's unlikely he would have founded Microsoft.

The positive side of the coin is that simply operating the computer -- as opposed to designing hardware or programming software -- gets easier with each passing day. A commonly held notion has it that females are more easily psyched out by the computer than men. Greta, a widowed neighbor of mine -- and former teacher no less -- stubbornly refuses to do e-mail with her grandson because she views the computer as being more scary than a rattlesnake with two heads. Too bad Rear Admiral Dr. Grace Murray Hopper is no longer around. She would set Greta straight in a hurry. Dr. Hopper received the Naval Ordnance Development Award for pioneering work on the early giant computers Mark I, Mark II, Mark III and

Univac when computers were <u>really</u> complex. In 1969, at age 63 she was awarded the first ever Computer Science Man-of-the-Year Award from the Data Processing Management Association. <u>Man</u> of the year! Male or female, she believed, a mind is a mind.

I tried to no avail to convince Greta that doing e-mail is far less complicated than baking one of her delicious chocolate cakes. Dr. Hopper would have done a better job.

Anyone who feels there's validity to the notion that women are less capable than their male counterparts to master computer technology can check this out easily enough. They need only call the customer support line of America on Line, Compuserve, or one of the other software service providers where they are as apt to hear a woman's voice at the other end as a man's. At Microsoft hundreds of Bill Gates's top rated technologists are -- you guessed it -- female.

Confront the Problem Head-on.

If technology torments have you tearing at your thinning hair several options make more sense than worrying about your real or assumed inadequacy. First, determine if your worry about the computer is a reasoned or unreasoned fear. I could cite more than one case where gutsy seniors resolved not to be cowed by computer phobia and, after a course or two coupled with a bit of hands-on training, found their fear converted to fascination.

A friend of mine, Joe Simmons, panicked when the outcome of a strategic planning meeting was a decision to automate his production management job. "I guess that means you'll be bringing in a computer expert," he told Charley Egan, his boss.

"Not necessarily. Your production and management savvy are more important to us than technology expertise. A couple of courses and I'm confident you'll take the technology in stride."

"You gotta be kidding," Joe replied. "I hate the damn computer. It's Greek to me."

"It was to me too at the outset," his boss said. "Give it a try. You have nothing to lose."

Joe enrolled in two courses sponsored by the company, an introductory course, and a basic class related to the work he was doing. "I was so intrigued by the introductory course," he says, "I couldn't wait for the second one."

Believe it or not, today my friend Joe is a computer aficionado. In addition to company sponsored courses, he takes advanced classes on his own. His goal is to qualify as a systems analyst. It's like any other change that takes place in your life. "Like Charley says," Joe concedes, "You never know until you give it a try."

Two or three decades ago in the workplace, mastering the computer meant one had to learn how to program it, a complicated procedure. Those days are long past. In most jobs, working with the computer today is child's play compared to what it was in the '60s and '70s.

In my experience, your first option when confronted with any kind of significant change is to give it your best shot rather than oppose and resist. Like Joe, you might even wind up liking it. There are few greater satisfactions than a tough challenge faced, struggled with, and overcame.

What If the Challenge Isn't for You?

Suppose, like some seniors, "trying it" doesn't work? What if, as is the case for many would-be contract bridge players, your mind is simply not geared to that kind of learning? On the job, I have learned you can determine this well in advance and make realistic plans to deal with it. Don't wait for Installation Day to decide you can't, or have no inclination to, cope with computer or other technology.

In the workplace, technology is rarely sprung overnight. The handwriting usually adorns the wall well in advance, and well in advance is when you should start planning for it. Psychologist Henry James said that attitude is more important than aptitude. Almost invariably your state of mind will determine the state you wind up in. Studies show that when one plans in advance, switching or losing a job often turns out more beneficial than catastrophic. Experience also proves that a change of career can be the most rewarding and exciting event of your life.

If you're plagued by technology you feel you're unable to or don't want to master, it's never too soon to review your options. (Like recruiting your ten year old grandson to give you some pointers.) There are probably more options than you imagine. There's no better time than now to start exploring them.

Dealing with Health Worries

The good news is that given the advances of medical and psychological science, age 70 today is the physical and mental equivalent of 50 or 55 a few decades ago. Nonetheless, in the department of valid concerns, health rates high. But from a What's-ahead? standpoint, in a sense it's often the easiest worry to deal with. Consider a typical case in point.

Alice Butler, an executive secretary, recently celebrated her 60th birthday. Alice has an assortment of ailments from arthritis to a "heart problem" that are not life threatening. Three years ago she realized she was approaching the point in her life where other things were more important to her than work, she tired more quickly, and her job attendance might no longer be exemplary. Looking and planning ahead, she decided it was time to start tapering down.

Smart lady, Alice. She also decided that the last way she wanted spend her senior years was vegetating around the condo pool, playing mah jong or bridge five days a week, or engaging in conversation no more stimulating than what was the "early bird" menu. On top of that, other interests -- the children, grandchildren, tennis, travel, and cultural pursuits -- now compete with her work as priorities.

But her job is important to her. It's often exciting and fun and provides the status she loves. So what to do? Alice thought, and again the key question: What are my options? Her first step was to define her objective: Taper down if possible to 15 or 20 hours per week instead of 37+. An experienced executive secretary in a specialized field, Alice saw two possible ways of achieving her goal. 1. Persuade her boss to gradually curtail her hours. 2. Seek part time work with another company.

Failing this, having the advantage of being financially comfortable, she would turn to volunteer work in the community. Screwing up her courage, Alice discussed her thoughts with her boss. "Let me think about it," he replied. Not wanting to lose a highly competent aide he had come to rely on, her boss complied.

Today Alice puts in an average of 15 hours a week and, though still aching and weary at times, she has a chance to grow old gracefully, and her health is no longer a worry.

What If You Have Life Threatening Health Problems?

We all know people with serious heart, cancer, or other afflictions who are nonetheless living normal and productive lives. One friend, who we all expected to die or become incapacitated years ago, is still hanging in there and defying the medical prognosis. All I can say from observation and experience is that whatever the diagnosis, remaining busy and active within prescribed medical and physical limitations, provides the best assurance of dignified longevity. Counsel beyond this point exceeds the expertise and scope of this book and would be most advisedly sought from health care professionals.

Are Downsizing Shakes Getting You Down?

They seem to be dropping like flies -- at Kodak, GM, IBM, AT&T, Citicorp -- all over the place. Call it "reengineering," "reduction in forces," "rightsizing," "downsizing," whatever. "Am I next?" is a question causing more gray hair these days than front line battle jitters. But say you're in your fifties or sixties, is the worry justified?

It depends. What it depends on is who you are, what you know, what you've done, and what you can still do. Also, most important, whether or not your state of mind is positive or negative. If you're fearful, it's negative. If you're "tuning out" because of frustration or disgust, it's negative. What I recommend you consider is this: How many plusses do you have working for you? Which is precisely what Jim Pankowitz did.

Jim, 58, employed by a large New York public relations agency, was sharp enough to read the proverbial handwriting on the wall. The firm's founder and CEO spent more time on the golf links than he did in his office and depended on his marginally competent son to run the business in his absence. The son listened to advice then did things his own way. Jim disagreed with the way some of the firm's major accounts were handled. He had ideas for bringing in new business. The suggestions for change he submitted months ago were still being "considered." In Jim's experience that meant shelved. Given the status quo, how secure was the firm's future? Not very, Jim believed, so he started baiting his hook.

Viewing his days as numbered, he started calling contacts he knew in the field. When this didn't work, he decided to start his own firm. But he didn't do it in one rash precipitous move. Applying his knowhow, and ideas his boss had shelved, he sold first one client then another. Four months later, as Jim had predicted, the downsizing axfell. With three clients already in his stable, he pretended dismay, but chuckled all the way home. Today Jim heads a small but growing public relations agency with one employee to date and soon hopes to close a contract with no lessan account than General Electric.

Moral of the story: Being downsized, given the right skills, savvy, and attitude, could be the greatest career building opportunity ever presented to you. Having been dealt a good hand, the next move is up to you.

Where and how else can you apply the expertise and skills developed over the years? What career or life change could you make that you always wanted to make, but never had the guts to pull off? Talk it over with family, friends, and associates. Examine your motivations and options as objectively as possible. Formulate a feasible plan for yourself. Throw up trial balloons. To the extent that you can, test your plan in advance as Jim did, before the fateful ax descends.

Don't Overlook That Unvoiced Anxiety?

You are approaching 60, 61, 62... and already having reached your peak you feel yourself slipping downward. Maybe you haven't articulated it to your spouse as yet, or even to yourself. But typically, if you are reading the signs it is it's in the back of your mind. Making it go away won't be easy. But if you can develop a mindset that will allow you to give that unvoiced anxiety the gate, it will be a milestone on your road to successful re-<u>fire</u>-ment.

Unvoiced but deeply felt nonetheless. What I refer to is your imminent loss of accumulated status, that feeling of importance you acquired after years of hard knocks, hard work, and achievement. Perhaps you rank among the top three on the sales force. Or head up a department. Or run your own operation. Or a group leader on the production line. Or you're a senior engineer in charge of twelve other professionals. Or vice president of this division or that.

The reality to face up to is that time forces change. Given the inevitability of change, maybe it's time to relinquish the vice presidency to a successor. Or to concede you are no longer the empowered high muckamuck you've become accustomed to being. Or face the realization that stepping down, or being forced to step down, in no way diminishes your real worth or competence. John Ruskin put it simply enough. "The first test of a truly great man is humility."

Maybe it's time for a bit of humility.

Change over which we have no control -- in response to age, market conditions, the economy, or whatever -- is going to happen like it or not. The smart approach is to anticipate and plan for it far in advance. The earlier you tune in and prepare to adjust, the less you will be shocked by a vanity jolt. Believe me, I speak from experience.

<u>Take Yourself Down a Peg or Two.</u> For years I was a vice president, then president, of Steelcraft Manufacturing Co. in Cincinnati, the metal door manufacturing company my dad and brother founded. In the eyes of hundreds of employees I was king of the hill. It was heady stuff. Until circumstances dictated we sell out to American Standard Inc. As part of the deal I became a vice president of American Standard. More heady stuff, except that I was in conflict with myself. I examined my situation and didn't know if I would enjoy working for a giant corporation. But what I did know was that as a frequent hotel guest during my business years the hotel industry had always intrigued me.

So, and as a backup plan for the future, soon after I started with American Standard I bought as an investment a Holiday Inn in South Florida. As time passed I decided that I did indeed enjoy my job at American Standard. I also enjoyed owning a hotel -- so much so that I built a second Holiday Inn. So, for years I was a vice president of American Standard <u>and</u> the owner of two hotels.

So far so good. But in time, because of a "reorganization," I was fired from American Standard. It didn't faze me a bit. I had done my homework and prepared well in advance. Instead of grousing and grieving, I decided to make the hotel business my career and built a third hotel, this time a Sheraton in Boca Raton Florida.

It's no secret that life and the marketplace are in perpetual flux. There are few constants we can depend on. With this reality in mind I volunteered to serve on the advisory board at Lynn University in Boca Raton and other South Florida educational institutions. Ten years later, when the hotel industry ran into hard times and the banks would not renew my mortgage I lost the hotels.

I didn't say, "No problem." But, however traumatic, I was ready for it. My planning discipline served me well. One of the key abilities I had going for me was my sales and marketing experience. Having qualified myself in advance, winning a vice presidency at Lynn as a fund raiser was no great undertaking. At age 72, that's what I'm doing today, never having missed a beat. Retirement? Ukh. The word never entered my mind.

All of this was a learning experience and I'm proud of the way I came through. In retrospect I'm proud I never responded to adversity with excuses or bitterness, and never groused or made excuses. I knew I was no less important and no less a manager, despite my fair share of goofs and misjudgments. Most significant, I feel myself more of a person for having honestly faced up to my defeats and defects. My friends are still friendly. My family still loves me. My neighbors and associates still respect me. And those who don't aren't worth worrying about.

A key point I want to make is that dealing with life's hard knocks is one of the greatest challenges we face. Anticipating and preparing for adversity is the only sensible way to respond to it.

Does the Prospect of Change Rattle You?

To paraphrase an old saw: If change is inevitable why not relax and enjoy it? That may be easier said than done. But I can say from experience it is easier to do when you plan for it.

Change like ice cream comes in a variety of flavors. The toughest kind to adapt to is the change that's imposed on you when you're not ready for it. The easiest kind is the kind you yourself initiate. The most successful kind of change you initiate is the kind you ponder and hammer out months or years in advance of the event.

Personalizing this problem, when and why should the need for change be of major concern?

- When an intolerable situation exists in your life or on the job.
- When problems develop that create personal hardship or financial loss.
- When a condition exists that threatens your health or safety.
- When frictions develop that trigger enmity or disruption at home or at work.
- When you find the status quo sapping the motivation and enthusiasm you once possessed in abundance.

Here's a classic case that occurred a few years ago in a New Jersey cosmetics plant. No one in the company was harder working or more conscientious than Bill Chernoff. At age 54 he had, in over twenty years, risen through the ranks to become production manager. No one was better at what he did than Bill, and he loved what he did.

Unfortunately, what Bill neglected to anticipate and act upon was the reality that, given the acceleration of change, 'what he was doing' would, before long, fail to meet the demands of the job. The plant was slowly automating a phase at a time. But Bill was too busy to take the time to qualify himself to deal with the emerging technology. Instead of preparing for it, he resisted it. A young computer-smart aide was brought in to fill the gap in Bill's knowhow. As the plant became more fully automated, the aide's role grew in importance. After six months on the job, he replaced Bill as department head. Bill shouldn't have been shocked, but when he was let go he was stunned and bitter.

It wasn't technology that defeated Bill; it was Bill. Major change rarely takes place overnight. Years before the inevitable transition was apparent, Bill had access to training opportunities. He didn't take advantage of them. Smart enough to win a key job, he had the overwhelming advantage of knowing the operation from A to Z. Why he didn't respond to the challenge -- or if unwilling to take on the technology, select another career for himself -- is hard to understand.

Change Your Mindset About Change. The good things in life don't come easy. A rule I try to adhere to is that the harder the goal, the greater the reward when you achieve it. People resist change because it makes them think hard and work harder. It disrupts their habit structure. The main reason people get rattled by change is because they wait too long to prepare for it.

Yet in life and on the job, the more change you are exposed to the more experience you accumulate, the more expertise you develop, the more you are worth to your boss and yourself, the more plusses you will have working for you in planning your options for the future.

Change will occur whether you like it or not. People change. Goals, and aspirations change. The marketplace and economy change, churned by new ideas and technology. In my experience, change is the most critical ingredient I could name of success, and successful planning. Diversification makes for a more interesting, productive, and exciting life. If you welcome change as a friend instead of something to worry about, you will cash in on its friendliness.

Is the Pressure Getting To You?

Pressure comes in two varieties: Helpful, and harmful. Pressure is helpful when it pumps up your adrenaline and makes you perform better, faster, or smarter. A classic example is the actor who experiences heightened tension when about to go on stage. Pressure is harmful though when, over aprolonged period, it tightens blood vessels and muscles and makes its victim neurotic.

If harmful pressure on the job or at home is getting you down, it's time for a planned and organized change.

Atlanta-based data processing manager George Etri, 56, was putting in an average of 60 to 70 hours a week, not because he wanted to, but because he felt the job called for it. The job pressure was bad enough. Even worse was his
wife Ethel's nagging. "This is no life," she kept griping continuously.

She had cause for complaint. Not only did George put in unreasonable hours, he often brought work home on weekends. Ethel's gripes were classic and common enough and so were the consequences.

- George's work overload was ruining their social life.

- It robbed the Etris of time with the family.

- The excessive workload was adversely affecting George's health.

- Ethel wanted more pleasurable time with her husband. She loved to dance. But George was usually too tired to do any thing after work, much less go dancing. He fatigued so much of the time, their sex life was languishing.

The need for change was apparent. When the problem reached the point where it threatened his marriage, George reluctantly decided he had to do something about it. But as he reasoned repeatedly with Ethel who kept pressuring him to change jobs, a data processing manager's job is hectic. It would be no less hectic in another company; the only thing a job change would accomplish is a cut in pay. So what to do?

In desperation Ethel urged, "At least talk to your boss, Harry. He might be able to help."

Bill sighed. "Okay, I'll talk to Harry."

"Ethel's driving me crazy," he told his boss.

When George explained why Harry was sympathetic. "I can understand how she feels," he said.

<u>Delegate Your Way To Good Health.</u> Ethel was right. Harry was well qualified to help and did so. George's boss reviewed his workload, piece by piece, project by project. Result, over a period of months, many of the tasks George formerly handled himself were delegated to trained and able subordinates. In addition, personnel shifts were made that further eased his workload. Today George carries a well balanced burden. The Etris marital and social life has improved dramatically.

How does planning for happiness and productivity in your senior years come into the picture? In George's situation his boss was as much to blame for the predicament as he himself was. Harry should have been aware of his manager's self-imposed workload and destructive schedule. With the need for change so apparent remedial action should have been taken months or years ago. But Harry isn't unique. Thousands of employees, executives and supervisors alike are overburdened and overstressed due to an absence of planned delegation.

A variety of causes from personality conflicts and unrealistic goals to arrogant and autocratic bosses and associates can produce unhealthful job pressure. But experience proves that in the majority of cases, where the

pressure on managers is created by work overload and excessive

35

hours, the reason boils down to a failure to delegate work and responsibility effectively, and to train subordinates to take over tasks they are doing themselves.

Happy Fourth of July!

So you got fired. Congratulations. Few people who get booted are in a frame of mind to consider and reflect on this. But whatever the date you get fired, you can think of that day as the Fourth of July. Independence Day! At long last, you've been cut free, free to spend the rest of your life in the glorious pursuits of your long time dreams and goals. Prepare for Independence Day well in advance, and you will know how to soar to new heights of achievement and pleasure.

Deciding to quit a job that for years provided income and security for yourself and your family can be a traumatic decision to make. But whether you liked the job or not, once you have been fired, the decision has been made for you. That can be good or bad, depending on who and what you are, and most of all your state of mind.

Studies show that getting fired is most often beneficial for planners and optimists, less often beneficial for pessimists. I know from experience that getting the ax can open the world of opportunity you have been secretly yearning for. As a highly successful executive friend of mine puts it, "Optimists don't worry about being fired. They're too busy planning their next move."

<u>Give Opportunity a Chance To Kick In.</u> Ask yourself, as I did when I lost my vice president's job at American Standard. "How can I turn this seeming adversity to my advantage?" As I have said, the hotel business had always intrigued me. Given the culture at American Standard and the marketplace tempo of the times, I had suspected that one day the ax would probably fall. I was thus well prepared in advance when it did.

I had devoted fruitful hours to study and evaluation of the hotel and restaurant business. I noted weaknesses in the way some hotels were run. I recognized the critical importance of superior service and its lack in many establishments. I had developed ideas with these thoughts in mind. When the time came I was ready. For years I ran three successful hotels and enjoyed the experience.

The crucial question to ask yourself when you are fired is: What do I have going for me that will make a new job or career as productive as the one I just lost?

The answer to this question is: <u>A lifetime of experience.</u> How often during your years on the job did you think of other things you might have been doing, other careers or opportunities you might have pursued? The ideal time to give vent to those musings is before the ax falls. Or, failing this, when it happens.

Are You in a Financial Bind?

If so, one thing is certain. Worrying about it won't make you more secure.

If you are in your 50s, 60s, or 70s, your financial status fits into one of three categories:

1. Hard pressed.
2. Comfortable.
3. Affluent.

How you rate yourself depends on your health, assets, investments, lifestyle, family educational and other commitments. Clearly, the person worth a million dollars in cash and other holdings -- with four or five grandchildren of college age to whom he has pledged support -- is less affluent than the person with comparable assets and minimal family commitments.

Generally speaking, if you are hard pressed financially, the plan for your senior years will have to include provisions for continuing income if and when you are "retired" from your present job.

"Comfortably" financially secure these days is rarely secure enough if you hope to enjoy your share of the glitter offered by the so-called golden years. If you fit into this category, you will need and want some kind of income in years to come.

If you're lucky enough to have wound up affluent in your 50s, 60s, or 70s, additional income -- given the tax and other consequences involved -- will probably be of minor importance. You may well, and hopefully, think in terms of enjoyable productive activity designed more to serve and help others than for the money unneeded, that you will receive.

Whether hard pressed, comfortable, or affluent, a subsequent chapter on financial planning will provide guidance in how most effectively to meet your re-_fire_-ment goals, whether income oriented or not.

Chapter 3

Map out your future

Defining Your Strengths and Weaknesses

"A man who does not think and plan long ahead will find trouble right at his door"

Confucius

Industrialist Charles Kettering put it even more succinctly: "I expect to spend the rest of my life in the future, so I want to be reasonably sure of what kind of future it is going to be. That is my reason for planning."

QUESTION: What has the future in store for you?

ANSWER: Precisely what you put in store for the future.

Your future will be bright if you take positive action to light it with brightening promise. It is a forgone conclusion that you can do anything you want if you have the will, the time, and the health to do it. The will is in your hands alone. The exciting news is that never before has the opportunity been greater to cash in on your built-in bonus of time and good health.

My friend and fellow writer Ray Dreyfack, who helped me with this book, conducted a little survey on his own. He spoke with a random sampling of 25 friends and neighbors, all of whom are over 70 years of age or older. Twenty of them, he learned, were older than one of their parents were when they died; 17 were older than both of their parents. This was only a mini poll, but I think it is representative. People are living longer, and will continue to live longer as living habits along with medical science keep improving.

39

Statistics from several insurance, government, and private organizations support this contention.

A reality gaining increasing recognition is that, keeping the four quadrants of one's lifetime in mind, three or four decades ago middle age was age 40; a couple of decades ago, middle age was age 50; today more often than not, 'middle age' comes at 60 or close to it.

On top of that, people are living healthier. Studies by the Rand Corporation and others show that problems among older people – *most dramatically among those over 80* – relating to eyesight, lifting, climbing and walking having declined significantly.
What's more, notes Rand researcher Vicki Freedman: "We know the elderly today are better educated than 10 years ago, and we know people with education are less likely to engage in unhealthy behaviors, and are more likely to see doctors."

So the stage is wide open. But nowadays 50 and 60 are a long way from 'elderly.' Since you will be living longer, you should start planning earlier.

Broaden Your Circle of Interests

No one said it was easy. But look back on your life. How many things in your experience that were really and truly worthwhile were easy to get or accomplish? Few if any. You could, of course, trust to luck. But Panhandlers Alley in Times Square, New York is crowded with unfortunates who trust to luck. From what I have learned, your chances are multiplied a hundred fold when you buckle up and bust your gut to get what you want. Even more important, I have learned that 'busting your gut' to get what one wants can be exciting and fun once you start getting it.

Experience proves that the surest and fastest way to expand your interests and opportunities is to BROADEN YOUR CIRCLE OF INTERESTS WHILE IN YOUR 50'S. With both income and outcome in mind. Whether you are out to make money, or have fun and excitement for yourself and your family, *diversification* is the magic key.

A doctor friend of mine has a lucky son. I'll call him Ralph. His dad would like nothing better than for him to become a doctor, but is by no means insisting. "It's your decision to make," he says. Ralph is bright, but ten years back had a problem common to young people today. Despite having obtained a degree from Yale, he didn't know what he wanted to do with the rest of his life. On top of that, he had become lazy. "'What I think had entered his mind', his dad told me, 'was to become a perpetual student'."

One day Ralph and his dad sat down for that inevitable talk. Ralph scratched his head. "I've been mulling over two options: Maybe take a few extra courses, you know, to broaden my education. Or maybe spend a year or so knocking around Europe and South America."

"What kind of courses?"

"I don't know. Maybe some more language, or cultural stuff." He had at one time shown an interest in a medical career but made no mention of it.

The doctor said, "Son, I'll finance your medical education, but I won't pay for random courses or trips abroad. If you do that, you're on your own."

Ralph frowned. "I'm not sure a medical career is for me, Dad."

His father shrugged. "That's your choice to make; but I don't think it's one you can keep putting off."

Within the next two or three weeks Ralph signed up for medical school. The point makes itself. Millions of people, not only young like Ralph, <u>but older folks like you and I as well</u>, suffer from the same *un*-occupational hazard. When it comes to the hard, tough decisions, we have to be prodded – by ourselves or by somebody else. Considering the alternatives, Ralph figured it would be harder to set out on his own, to either finance his continuing 'education,' or to embark on a year of adventure and travel, than to get on with his life.

Dad's constrictions gave him the firm but gentle prod he needed. Had he acceded to the boy's wishes he would have done neither himself nor his son a favor.

Harry's experience was all the prod Ed Holding needed. A highly specialized public relations executive with proven managerial skills and specialized knowledge of environmental pollution control, at 56 Ed was financially comfortable. A key part of his job was writing press releases, stockholder reports, and features for the company magazine. He was good at his job, but had been doing it so many years he was just about fed up with it.

A talented musician, Ed also liked to play basketball and duplicate bridge. But pressured by the long hours his job demanded, he found himself neglecting his family and ignoring the interests he loved. Ed knew what he wanted most. He wanted to write, not releases and reports, but books. Since he couldn't dismiss money entirely, his burgeoning plan had two books in mind: a business book for the money it would bring, the novel to cater to a lifelong dream. That's where Harry comes into the picture. Ed knew Harry well; he used to work with the guy. He knew he could write rings around Harry, and he knew he was a whole lot smarter and more technically knowledgeable. Harry was making out as a writer. *If Harry can do it*, Ed reasoned, *so can I.*

He could, and he did. Ed knew that from a money standpoint, writing the novel would be a long shot. He couldn't do that without planning the business book and clinching a contract for it. Today he is working on both, and has other projects in mind. The frosting on the cake is that he has plenty time for basketball, and more than enough for his family.

Experiment, Then Evaluate Your Progress – Again And Again

Whatever one's age, the natural tendency is to follow the path of least resistance, *unless* we force ourselves into a habitual mindset – as we recommend – of seeking new challenges and opportunities at every turn. What works best in my experience is to keep trying new ideas, new activities, new projects over and over again, and following every experiment, **evaluate**. What did I get out of it? Was my contribution worthwhile? Was it appreciated? Was it rewarding financially, socially, psychologically? Do I want to keep doing it again and again and again? Experiment, review, assess and revise. Do this often enough *throughout your life* and you will no problem deciding what is most worthwhile and fulfilling.

Try what? You pays your money and you takes your choice. We are each one of us different. What appeals to you won't necessarily appeal to me or the next guy.

Depending on your age, occupation, economic status, family commitments, personal likes and dislikes, take a stab at what might interest you. Do you enjoy your job more than any other kind of work you could imagine or qualify for? How might you feel about continuing as self-employed instead of job holder? Do you want to keep on being gainfully employed after being 'retired,' downsized, or voluntarily throw in the sponge? What about volunteer work? The field is wide open, the need ever-increasing in the fields of health care, education, community programs, entertainment and politics where opportunities abound to use the skills you already have. What 'grabs' you the most? My personal experience has taught me that broadening one's vistas -- which automatically adds excitement and zest to one's life -- is not an either-or proposition. You can be employed full time as I am and still handle six or sixteen outside activities. I couldn't begin to tell you how many boards and committees I serve on – and the satisfaction and pleasure I get from every one of them.

The Magic E

I'm not talking about E-mail, although that is magic enough. I'm talking about what Ralph Waldo Emerson refers to as "the mother of effort". **ENTHUSIASM!**

The more activities, projects and pursuits you experiment with, the greater your variety of choices will be when decision time rolls around. The question, of course, will be *which* of your many activities will be Choice No. 1 for your rekindlement years. Your selection – at least at the outset – will be much easier to make if , one by one, you subject your various options to a personalized L/E (Level of Enthusiasm) test.

The L/E test is best scheduled on two separate days, preferably a week apart, and is easy to take.

STEP ONE – On a sheet of blank paper make a list of all viable options that come to mind – work for pay, work to pay your social dues, educational pursuits, recreational activities, health-building projects – anything that will take a significant amount of time on a day to day basis.

STEP TWO – Run off an exact copy of your list and put it aside.

STEP THREE – On a scale of 1 to 10 apply a Level of Enthusiasm rating to each entry on your original list. In short, what you feel at that moment you would like to devote a major part of your time doing in the days and months ahead. Enter that number alongside of your entry.

STEP FOUR – A week or so later, without consulting your filled-out list, apply a second set of ratings to your duplicate copy.

STEP FIVE – Compare the two lists. Where your original and new L/E ratings don't coincide, decide what your true rating should be and make the adjustment.

STEP SIX – Show your adjusted list to your spouse and say, Joan, or John, "What do you think of my choices?"

If your spouse agrees you're ahead of the game. If agreement isn't reached, the next step is the most important and most fun of all. Talk it out. Review the pros and cons. Exchange your opinions and preferences and finally, hopefully, you will see eye to eye. A major key to success is flexibility. Since your spouse will be a major party to your rekindlement plan, he or she should play a major role. Seek advice, yes. But never forget that the buck stops with you. And don't lose sight of Jimmy Carter's insightful comment that what's best about being old is…

...the complete freedom you have to make decisions about what you will do and how your will spend the rest of your life.

This holds especially true in your 5-'s and 60's when the time is at hand to pursue the career you want to try next.

'Freedom' includes freedom to experiment with and develop new enthusiasms. While you may have an educated idea out of your experience what already fires you up with excitement, but you probably have little if any idea about the potential of projects and activities you have not tried to date. This would include scores of endeavors, voluntary and otherwise, that are entirely new to you.

I know a 61 year old woman who, once she became deeply involved into the Pro Life/Freedom of Choice debate – I won't mention on which side – her personality changed from dismal and dull to highly spirited and brimming with life and energy. A 58 year old man I know was similarly transformed when he joined the gun control battle. Prior to that, his life was so flat simply looking at him could make one yawn. His involvement made his emotions spring to life if nothing else. At least now he hated Charleton Heston and Tom Selleck.

Endless transformations could be cited in response to renewed involvement with the Internet, teaching kids to say no, coaching teen teams of all kinds, doing library work and – you could probably add as many items to his list as I can.

Having planned and considered, once you pinpoint the highest ranked activities on your L/E list you can indulge in these pursuits either on your own, or in conjunction with your live-in friend or spouse. Later on, if either or both of you decide to switch and try something else, as Jimmy Carter says, you will have the blessed **freedom** to do so.

Pinpoint Your Strengths and Weaknesses

If your objective is to energize your lifestyle, my strong conviction is that you are never too young or too old. I believe that a project I have in mind can work as well for seniors in the second and third quadrants of their lives as it can for first graders. The project, funded by a grant and conducted in conjunction with South Florida's Lynn University, is titled "Electronic Personal Portfolio."

The concept is as simple as it is powerful. The project starts in first grade. Young participants are equipped with computers and cameras in the classroom. It is the kids' responsibility, with assistance, of course, to gather their own electronic historical data, a complete personalized record of significant events in their school lives developed from 1st to 12th grades – speeches given, grades and awards, roles in school plays, special functions, parent-teacher visits, etc. The Portfolio will go with the children up until the time they graduate. Indexing of progress and development will be useful not only for college admission, but will be an invaluable analytical tool for both parents and teachers, and most of all for the kids themselves.

I see no reason why this Personal Portfolio idea wouldn't be as conceptually adaptable to *anyone* who is embarked on one of the most important plan-alytical experiences in his or her lifetime. Experimentally, I tested the idea on my own lifetime of corporate work, volunteer work, and recreation and found it highly instructive. **Especially instructive in pinpointing my strengths and weaknesses.**

What did I learn from my years of managerial experience? From my years of running a manufacturing company? From my service on innumerable community boards and committees? Where was I strong? Where was I weak? What did I enjoy the most? What, if anything, could I have lived without? From which activities did I derive the greatest rewards, financial, spiritual, and simple just feeling good about it? What smart moves and/or mistakes were particularly instructive? What assets have I to show for all my hard work and effort, non-financial as well as financial? How much friendship; how much family love and devotion?

Think about it. What better tool could one pick to help analyze and plan for re-**RIRE**-ment?

Help Wanted - Experts

Today's want ads for desirable jobs may not be stated in exactly this way, but that is what they say nonetheless. Like it or not, more often than not, qualifying as an expert implies a working familiarity with the computer. The more the familiarity, the greater the expertise. This doesn't always apply – many skills don't involve the computer – but it applies often enough to make one sit up and take notice.

Search consultant Nick Corcodilos of Lebanon, N.J. lays it on the line bluntly enough. "Employers are looking for very specific job skills and capabilities and turning away people en masse who don't have them."

Alex Berner, 54, thought his broad management experience and background combined with general educational credentials would be more than adequate to relocate quickly when he decided to chuck the longtime job he no longer could stomach. To his surprise he learned it was anything but. "I was getting positive feedback," he recalls, "but employers didn't know what to do with me. I had deep managerial skills but my broad knowledge of the computer didn't apply specifically enough to my work."

Today Berner is still plugging away at his old job, and taking a couple of advanced computer courses to qualify for the 21st century. Then he'll try again.

The good news is that if you have worked at diversified jobs and businesses all your life you already *are* an expert at one thing or another, if not several lines of work. The harder to take news is that you may have to sharpen your expertise if you haven't done so recently. The world is changing so fast that, especially if your livelihood is at issue, you cannot afford to stand still. Developing and/or upgrading your computer skills is probably the most glaring example applicable to thousands of people. In your particular line of work there may be others.

Selling oneself on the job market today can be compared to selling an article to a national magazine. Mailing your manuscript broad shot to 20 markets will almost certainly result in 20 rejection slips. Same thing applies to attempting to sell your services to 20 companies at once. The more effective strategy would be to target your job search on one or two prospective employers, then research the special needs of these companies, determine what is needed to fulfill them, and equip yourself to fill the bill. In most cases, as you get older it makes sense to accept less pay. What's most important is to settle on a career choice that will keep you dynamic and active.

Alice Dock, 58, a Pittsburgh housewife, did just that. Her kids long gone, she was bored with 'housewifing,' and decided to venture back into the job market. With 30 years as an executive secretary behind her, she started to apply for secretarial jobs. By her eighth polite rejection she got the message. Her experience was dated, but in form not substance. So she had a talk with her daughter-in-law who worked for a senior vice president of a large Pittsburgh company. Her information was in essence her own job description. Step one and most important, the old bugaboo: She would have to upgrade her computer skills; knowing how to do E-mail wasn't enough. Alice brushed up on the word processor, took a course in the local community college, studied the special needs of three companies in the area, and within four months was employed.

Finally, in calculating your strengths on the job market or in community service, don't sell short one of your most powerful assets of all: YOUR AGE. A growing number of employers are coming to realize these days that older employees are:

…in general harder working than their younger counterparts.
…more reliable, likely to attend and show up on time more regularly.
…skilled in training and mentor roles.
…less needful of fringe benefits.
…likely to bring experience and new perspectives to the job.
…less likely to encounter problems with their children that interfere with their work.
…less likely to complain about income or job conditions.
…less likely to become pregnant.

…willing to settle for less money.

…more willing to travel, both at home and abroad.

Never before -- especially in a booming economy with a growing scarcity of skilled reliable workers nationwide – has the recruitment and hiring of older workers been so active. Conclusion: Whatever your preference, they are out there waiting for you.

When it's time to step down

Let's get one thing straight. If it is time to step down, that doesn't mean it is time to bow out. Failing to differentiate between the two could be one of the biggest mistakes you might ever make. The challenge is to determine *in advance* what you are going to step down *to*. Golf? Cards? Travel? 'Relaxation?' Shuffling your stock holdings around? Or more challenging pursuits?

A key point to remember is that many people who were active in business most of their lives cannot simply suddenly pull out the stops and fold up. As they select new careers in their 50's or 60's, they certainly do not need high tension jobs. But they do need a degree of pressure and responsibility to prove to themselves and to others that they are still *in the game* and resolved to remain there for some years to come.

Example One – John Roth, 77, owned a small but successful advertising agency. His son Steve, a senior vice president – the *only* senior vice president – was his number two man. Steve had a lot of good ideas which, month after month, were being dumped on the shelf because Dad found it hard to break old habits. A bright guy, Steve's level of frustration reached the breaking point. When he informed Dad he was quitting, John could scarcely hide his shock. He stammered, he spluttered. "Why…!" "Dad, I think you know why."

They talked it out. Steve agreed to stay – under one condition. The agency would be *his* show as had long been promised. Dad agreed. "I can still give you help when it's needed." "Right, but only when it's needed, *and only if I ask for it.*"

So John Roth stepped down, and *almost* stepped out. Fortunately, Mildred couldn't stand having him around the house and prodded him into participating on half a dozen committees, boards, and professional organizations he long had expressed interest it. In his spare time – what little he has left – he teaches a course at a nearby university.

Example Two – Mary M.'s health could have been better. But that wasn't her main problem. What bugged her most was that at age 63, as a commercial artist employed by a publishing firm, she felt that 40 hours per week was too much for her. On top of that, she figured that if she didn't try a shot at some more serious art work, she would never do it. Ideally, she would have preferred resigning so she could spend most of her time painting, but she couldn't afford a full income loss. Wisely, she talked it over with her boss, the head of the art department.

"Mary, I don't want to lose you. How can I help?"

"Easy. You could cut my hours in half."

It was the shortest response she ever got in her life. "Done."

Example Three – Bob Kreissman, 74, was financial vice president of a profitable Westchester County, N.Y. men's toiletries company. He worked too hard and too long. His wife Dorothy complained that he didn't take enough time off, and Bob was beginning to feel the same way himself. It was time to step down. His smart boss prescribed no age limit for his high level executives. But how does one step down from a job he loves? Bob's answer was as simple as it was unusual. He delegated a significant part of his work to subordinates. He assured his boss, who was ten years his senior, that he would always be on hand and on call when urgently needed, and requested permission to arrange his own curtailed work schedule as he saw fit. In response he suggested cutting his salary in half. The arrangement worked out without a hitch.

How does a busy vibrant individual step down from a dynamic and exciting job without risking a life of sudden and abrupt inactivity? All it takes are equal doses of imagination, initiative, and gumption. Often it is largely a matter of time. The person is no *less* active; he is simply active less of the time. He grinds down on a gradual basis. Comes to work later, takes a longer lunch hour, leaves early. But while he's on hand, he *acieves!*

Give Boredom the Boot - Diversify

Author Saul Bellow defines boredom as 'the shriek of unused capacities.'

Norman Mailer carried it a step further when he decreed that "boredom slays more of existence than war."

Some people, seniors and otherwise, always seem to be bored.

Some don't give themselves the *time* to be bored, having planned in advance what they will do *not* to be bored. My wife Phyllis and I count ourselves among the lucky ones who fall into this category. I cannot recall myself *ever* being bored except rarely when forced into conversation with people who like to talk but have nothing to say. I'm sure Phyllis would echo this sentiment.

We are almost never bored because of the vast variety of activities in which we engage; perhaps, equally important, the variety of new and different activities we tend to enjoy.

"Strangers In the Night" – or Day

A few weeks ago we were invited to a dinner party. "Bob, I must apologize," the hostess said. "The other guests will all be strangers."

"Great!" I replied, "that's an added plus. Phyllis and I love to go to parties, or meetings, or on vacation, where we encounter strangers, where we don't know a single soul. The level of interest automatically rises."

So many people are afraid of that. I sometimes wonder why. Is it because they are shy, insecure? I find it exciting to meet new people. I play a game with myself when I do. Who are they? What do they do? What do they like and dislike? What do we have in common? Can I help them in some way? Can they help me in some way?

You don't need a psychologist to tell you that the principal ingredient of boredom is the day to day sameness and repetition. Repetition is the gas that fuels burnout. Upon starting a new job or project, can you ever recall being bored? It's doubtful. Something new may make you apprehensive or fearful, even annoyed. But never bored.

Dale Carnegie said: "Are you bored with life? Throw yourself into some kind of work you believe in with all your heart, live for it, die for it, and you'll find a happiness that you thought could never be yours."

'Work' cannot be too broadly translated. It could mean physical labor, the mental task of solving a problem or meeting a challenge, athletic or recreational activity that gives you genuine satisfaction and joy. What follows is a short Boredom Assessment Quiz tailored to your own personal situation and lifestyle. Answer each question as honestly and objectively as possible. Then score yourself at the end.

	YES	NO
1. Do you watch a lot of TV and frequently switch channels?	____	____
2. Do you believe you possess all the energy you need?	____	____
3. Are you an advocate of continuous learning?	____	____
4. Are you often restless and edgy?	____	____
5. Do you exercise briskly and regularly?	____	____
6. Are you usually agreeable when something new is suggested?	____	____

7. Do you enjoy meeting new people?   ____ ____

8. Do you often have free time on your hands?   ____ ____

9. Do you get more sleep than you need?   ____ ____

10. Do you do too many things
"just to keep occupied"?   ____ ____

Total Score   ____

Do you have the demon **boredom** pretty much under control? Calculate your score to find out: On Questions 1, 4, 8, 9 and 10, give yourself 10 points for each NO answer; On Questions 2, 3, 5, 6, and 7, score 10 points for each YES answer. Now enter your Total Score below.

How did you fare? If your score is 80 or higher, congratulations; you have boredom pretty well under control. Sixty or 70 is fair but could stand a lot of improvement. Any score below 60 indicates that the **demon** seems to be dragging you down and calls for drastic remedial action as prescribed in this book.

Select "Can-Do" Role Models

This is the easy part: A remedy for boredom, and a prescription for renewal that has worked for innumerable men and women approaching the third and fourth quadrants of their lives. To help give you direction, inspiration, and motivation, pinpoint an individual – celebrity or otherwise – whom you greatly admire, and whose courage and lifestyle you would like to emulate. Consider the following examples in the light of your own personal situation, preferences, and needs.

John Bisch –This is not for everyone, but it was for Mr. Bisch and is a rekindlement option worth considering. "Companies Send Intrepid Retirees to Work Abroad," headlines a *Wall Street Journal*

53

article by Joannn S. Lublin. Whirlpool, Quaker Oats, and others have begun tapping a vast pool of retired employees for hard-to-fill temp jobs abroad. Stints usually run about six months or so. Mr. Bisch, a maintenance engineer from Marion, Ohio, wound up in Beijing, China where Whirlpool was in the process of closing down a refrigerator factory. Having ended a 37-year career with Whirlpool in 1995, he had no trouble recalling manufacturing techniques. A hell of an experience and a hell of an adventure. Are you bored? Do you have an adventuresome spirit? If this is your cup of tea, have a sip.

Walter Cronkite – Experience proves that as we mature our concerns and interests will broaden if we permit them to do so. Few demonstrate this better than "America's Most Trusted Anchorman." Today, 17 years after relinquishing the mike at CBS Evening News, Cronkite at age 81 is as articulate and spirited as ever on the changes in the print and electronic media of the world at large. The strong opinions expressed in his book, "A Reporter's Life," will inspire any doubters who think they are too old to plan new pursuits and new commitments. Did you make a significant contribution in your lifetime? Take a page from Cronkite's book. Talk about it. Write about it.

Elsie McDermott – After 34 years as an office manager for a New York textile importing company, 62 year old Mrs. McDermott, recently widowed, said she never wanted to see the inside of an office again. "Not that I didn't enjoy my job; but enough is enough." Still, people who are dynamic and blessed with healthy curiosity about life and its vicissitudes, are unwilling to settle down quietly and become part of the vegetation. Mrs. McDermott spent some of her time doing church and community work helping others. But determined to help herself too, she set off on an "extended education" jaunt two years ago, and has been 'jaunting' ever since – from Elderhostel to Elderhostel and from one senior education program to another, and from state to state. She has racked up 23 "learning experiences" in two years and says she is "just getting started and having a ball." Someone, she adds, once said, "you are never bored when you're learning."

John McMurray – "It's a culture all its own," McMurray, 63, told an Associated Press reporter. "You have to live it to appreciate it." The McMurrays appreciate it. One month in Augusta, Ga., another time in Scottsdale, Ariz., or Harrisburg, Pa., or Canton, Miss., another time, you name it. They own a 33-foot recreational vehicle which they use to travel to craft shows and festivals where they exhibit and sell a fine line of handmade silver jewelry. What a great way to earn a living! How many kindred spirits and friends have they made along the way? It would take a dozen address books to list them all. The McMurrays! Bored? Hey, you gotta be kidding.

Dr. Grace Murray Hopper – Born in 1906, Dr. Hopper died in 1992. In between, she stirred up a stew or two and won national recognition as one of the 20th century's ranking female achievers. A Vassar graduate in mathematics and physics, she went on to earn a Yale masters and doctorate. Married and childless – her husband died in 1945 – she served as an associate professor at Vassar until she was called upon to join the United States Naval Reserve to assist her country in its wartime challenges. Within time she advanced to the rank of Admiral. She kept working well into her eighties, "retired" with the rank of Rear Admiral, and is credited for having contributed significantly to the transition from primitive programming techniques to the use of sophisticated compilers. A true visionary, Admiral Hopper received numerous medals including the Naval Ordnance Development Award for her pioneering work on the Mark I, Mark II, and Mark III computers. Want a role model to emulate? Check out Admiral Hopper on the Internet as an example of what a senior can do when she puts her mind to it.

Margaret Dixon – Set yourself a tough challenge and renewal and rekindlement will come in its wake. Margaret Dixon didn't exactly plan it that way, but that's the way it worked out. In fact, she didn't have to plan it that way. "I like to be busy," she says. Many people, like Dr. Dixon, wouldn't have it any other way. They are the lucky ones. It's the folks who mindlessly settle into a deep-sinking rut who have the hardest problems to overcome. Margaret

Dixon knows about busy from way back. She taught elementary school, worked with disadvantaged children, ran a computer-assisted learning program for New York City's public school system, served as assistant principal, and then principal. Just to mention a small sampling of her busy work. So it was no surprise when Dr. Dixon and her husband, getting on in years but not in motivation, plunged into volunteer work as tutors, meals-on-wheels providers, and other activities. Don't leave yet. We're not finished. In 1988, a friend volunteered Dr. Dixon for an assignment as minority-affairs spokesperson for the American Association of Retired Persons. Hopefully, she can work with us in an effort to get AARP to change its name to the Association of Re-**FIRED** Persons.

We can all take a lesson from Dr. Dixon and others like her. The secret, if you have been busy all your life, is to take care not to *stop* being busy for any prolonged period of time. There's nothing wrong with short lapses of relaxation and idleness. We all need a second wind from time to time. But if you permit it to deteriorate into a habit, inertia may step in to take over.

Chapter 4

Explore exciting new possibilities

Reviewing and Refining Your Life Plan

"Most people would succeed in small things if they were not troubled by great ambitions."
Henry Wadsworth Longfellow

Frank was an Irish immigrant kid, discharged in 1953 after a two-year stint in the U.S. Army. Desperate to boost his income and status, he loaded sides of beef in a back-breaking job. But without a high school diploma, what chance did he have? He won admittance to NYU on probation, received the education credits needed, and embarked on a 30-year career as an English teacher in New York City vocational and high schools. After that, what was left? Retirement? Not for Frank.

The kids he taught had been intrigued by the stories of his impoverished childhood in Ireland. If he could teach English, he reasoned, he could write English. So he set to work on a new career. Well past middle age, **Frank McCourt's** book, *Angela's Ashes*, became an overnight best seller, and he is hardly through yet. We are the product of our life's experiences, McCourt believes. It is never too late to convert retiring to refiring.

If there is one characteristic of this author's makeup and personality that breathes into every sentence and word of his book it is enthusiasm, the old tried and true gung ho factor. I challenge readers to review and assess the nature and disposition of virtually any

57

successful person they could name, and I'll bet a case of scotch against a six-pack of beer they will find one thing in common: **ENTHUSIASM.**

No one said it was easy. To understate the case, training oneself to be gung ho is about as tough as it gets. But if you equate the degree of enthusiasm you display with the measure of success you hope to achieve, the good sense of the effort becomes clear. As experience proves, the two factors work together. They are complementary. Effort with one's success goal in mind breeds enthusiasm. Enthusiasm in its turn inspires effort. The two are an unbeatable combination.

Good Servant, Poor Master

P.T. Barnum said it all when he wrote that, "Money is a terrible master but an excellent servant."

Servant or master? The choice is yours.

It would be hard to undersell the material and psychological benefits money can buy. At the same time it is important to take care in the acquisition of money not to lose sight of the good things that money *can't* buy.

How much is enough? Nobody knows. You won't get the answer that applies specifically to you from any book, TV documentary, or guru.

As we grow older concerns about having enough money tend to increase. And increase, and increase, even far beyond our resources. We worry. What if I get sick and am no longer employable? What if I die; will my spouse be able to survive financially? Will we lose the house? Will there be enough to cover the kids' education? How secure does one have to be to enjoy financial security? A mindlessly assumed need to accumulate more and more can become irrational. The amassment of dollars can become a destabilizing obsession. We can all call to mind anecdotal evidence of this sad reality.

The case of – I'll call him Bill Jones -- stands out sharp and clear. Bill owned a small to midsize public relations firm in New York

City. He was a workaholic, his ten to twelve hour per day efforts targeted on the twin objectives of building his agency and accumulating wealth. In Bill's mind, his wife lived the "good life," drove a Porsche, had access to a lovely summer home in the country, was outfitted and bejeweled to the nines. What else could she want? The three Jones kids attended high priced schools. When they came of age they had pricey cars. No one could accuse Bill of being anything but a good provider. The key question here is: Provider of what?

The benefits of Bill Jones's financial success were abundantly clear in his mind. Sadly *unclear* were the *nonfinancial* benefits he had missed out on for most of his life. His wife didn't divorce him. Both she and her lover, also a family man, agreed there was no need for this. His 'well provided for' children hardly knew him. When Bill Jones died at age 68, he was mourned by his family, but all too superficially. He was worth $53 million in cash and securities. But what was he worth in love? In spiritual understanding and satisfaction?

One more time: How much is enough? Was $53 million enough for Bill Jones? You decide. He died a lonely, prematurely old man.

Escape from Affluenza

"Contact with nature. Human relationships. Creative activities. Isn't this, rather than money, what brings joy to our lives?" Humberto Cruz poses the question in an article for Florida's *Sun-Sentinel.*

That, adds Cruz, is one of the points most persuasively made in *Escape from Affluenza*, a one-hour documentary broadcast hosted by Scott Simon that appeared on public television stations nationwide. The program, Cruz says, "was a follow-up to a documentary about the *Epidemic of Stress*, overwork, shopping and debt caused by the dogged pursuit of the 'American Dream' which has been twisted to mean the acquisition of more and more material goods."

It's no coincidence that both documentaries appeared on and

around the July 4th weekend, which has been declared by co-producer Vivia Boe, to be "Independence from Stuff" week.

While, on the one hand, survey results show that most Americans concede they buy more 'stuff' than they need, a majority state they would be willing to reduce material possessions and income if it would mean spending more time with the family, and offer an opportunity to reduce stress.

So we repeat, with these thoughts in mind, how much do you need?

In his book, *The Silicon Boys, Newsweek* writer David A. Kaplan, defines bucolic Woodside as the "Silicon Valley's seat of power" where most homes sit on three to five acre lots. Here, Kaplan describes such extravagances as $18-a-pound ostrich salami, an Oracle engineer's ex-wife strutting 48 rack *feet* of clothing, $200-a-bottle balsamic vinegar, an applicant denied residency by the building department because a shower ledge was two inches too high, $50,000 Microsoft-bashing parties, and $3,900 lobster meals flown in from Maine. Not to mention astronomical restaurant tabs and mementos of dubious value auctioned off for five and six figure tabs.

Such are the materialistic excesses of cyber geeks and *nuveau riche* 20-and-thirty somethings, who dedicate 70 to 80 hour work weeks to the accumulation of wealth and – what else? What actual *values*? Family, community, pursuits of the heart and the mind? Are genuine family relationships possible in such circumstances? Cruz for one seems to doubt it. I for one seem to agree with him.
I kicked this around with a friend the other day who scrapes by contentedly at age 68 with a modest bank account and annual income of $48,000. "Do you envy these guys their seemingly unlimited wealth?" I asked.
He chuckled in response. "I envy them their brilliance and creative ingenuity. But I feel sorry for them if the Mercedes, million dollar chateaux, and ten thousand dollar pool parties are all they get out of it."

In his article, Cruz cites Seattle's Ron Simmons who left a lucrative job at Microsoft to pursue his dream of becoming an actor.

Simmons now has time to help others, Cruz reports. He's a Big Brother volunteer; he reads to the blind, and works with patients at an AIDS hospice. Can you measure the reward Simmons gets from his contribution against the pleasures of being able to throw a $10,000 pool party designed to show the competition how rich and famous you are?

No way! Ask Simmons. Ask Ed Ruskin. Ruskin, 56, quit a six-figure job to purchase, remodel, and resell two or three homes a year which cuts his income by two-thirds, but gives him time for the family, the game of tennis he loves, and volunteer work in the community. Ask Jan Bellinsky, 59, who turned down a high level executive job that would have given her 'stuff' by the closetful, but little time for her beloved music, theatre, and grandkids, and no time at all for community service.

Face the Practical Realities

What if you're down-sized at age 50, 54, or 60? A fat bankroll and hefty portfolio can ease the transition from your day job to whatever new life you choose. No argument there. But more and more folks in their 50's and 60's, according to recent *Modern Maturity, Wall Street Journal,* and other surveys and polls, ARE COMING TO REALIZE that at least as important as having enough money to spend is having enough time to spend on the things you want to do and the people you want to do them with..

What the battle for life's fulfillment boils down to as you approach your 50's, 60's, and 70's, is a balancing act between two of the most important bottom lines of your life – the *bottom line* on your financial balance sheet, and the bottom line on your style-of-life balance sheet.

Keeping in mind your age, health, family responsibilities, and societal obligations,
at what level of financial security can you afford to shift your focus from making more money to making more people love and appreciate you? The following 10 questions may help you decide.

Consider each question thoughtfully; jot down your answers as honestly and objectively as possible. Then score yourself in the end.

Your Personal Values Self-Audit

1. If you were faced with a moral dilemma, would you come to someone like yourself for advice, or go elsewhere?

2. What gives you more real enjoyment: depositing $1,000 to your account, or helping a friend out of a spot?

3. Do you spend more time on the phone talking with your broker, or with family members?

4. Most people say prayers. Are most of your prayers for yourself or for others?

5. Do you calculate your net worth frequently or every once in a while?

6. Do you have disturbing dreams often or rarely?

7. Do neighbors and associates come to you for help and advice often or infrequently?

8. If you won a sweepstake ticket would you spend most of the money on yourself, or on others?

9 Do you wear a bright friendly smile on your face often or rarely?

10. Does a stranger's traumatic experience ever move you to tears, or does it usually leave you indifferent?

How do your spiritual values stack up against your material values? Let's find out. Enter the following scores based on your answers.

1. If you answered yourself, score 10; others, score 0.
2. $1,000, score 0; help friend out of a spot, score 10.

3. Broker, score 0; family, score 10.

4. Yourself, score 0; others , score 10.

5. Once in a while, score 10; frequently, score 0.

6. Often, score 0; rarely, score 10.

7. Often, score 10; infrequently, score 0.

8. Yourself, score 0; others, score 10.

9. Often, score 10; rarely, score 0.

10. Tears, score 10; indifferent, score 0.

Add up the total of 10's that you entered. A score of 80 or higher indicates that your Spiritual Values IQ is high. Sixty or 70 means you are probably better than average. A score of 50 or lower indicates on the one hand that you are honest with yourself, and on the other that a bit of serious thinking about the true values of life is in order.

"Four Awesome Volunteers"

AARP's *Modern Maturity* magazine recently honored four winners in a field of thousands who demonstrated by means of constructive contribution and sacrifice the spiritual importance and individual reward one derives out of service to others.

Arlene Shipley, Jacksonville, Florida. Herself abused as a child, Shipley at 52 devotes full time and hard effort to her start-up of AngelAID, a volunteer-and-donation-based organization that provides free medical treatment, counseling, activities, and guidance for children who have been sexually abused, suffer a terminal illness, or are otherwise at risk.

Dee Deems, Albany, Oregon. Deems, 70, serves as the unpaid, full-time director of the Partnership for Housing, dedicated to the development of low-income housing for people in need. With the help of donated office space, state grants and loans, and local homebuilders, and voluntary effort by local citizens, hundreds of units are being developed.

Betty J. Frey, Navajo country, Arizona. At age 85, Frey volunteers her services initiating, and now supervising, the Tucson Adult Literacy Volunteers, one of the city's leading literacy centers. After long years of teaching English as a Second Language to hundreds of students, she continues to work hard to develop in other teachers the skills she herself has so masterfully achieved.

Irving A. Fradkin, St. Peter, Minnesota. A fervent believer in education, over the years Fradkin founded the National Dollars for Scholars program, and the Citizens' Scholarship Foundation of America. Recently, at age 78, he initiated a new program called The American Dream Challenge which provides scholarships for elementary school children with funding continued until the recipients finish high school. Provisions are then made for a link with the Dollars for Scholars program for further college education sponsorship.

Now weigh the joys and satisfactions of this inspiring volunteer foursome against those derived by money-centered individuals who devote so much of their effort to the accumulation of wealth they have little if any time left for anything else. Who do you think are actually "richer" in the really *significant* assets of life? One would have no choice in my opinion but to rank the wealth builders a poor second in the battle for lifestyle fulfillment and a warm welcome by St. Peter or his kosher counterpart.

Have You Considered Your Options?

If you are past 50 and haven't considered and planned your later life options and strategies, you are already late at the starting gate. The good news is that the number of exciting new possibilities is limited only by your imagination and research. Today employment options, especially in technology, are growing faster than crab grass in an untended lawn. The bad news is that despite so many *unforeseen* possibilities out there for the taking, it doesn't occur to most people to review or explore them. An added plus for the adventuresome.

THERE'S NO WAY OF KNOWING WHAT THE CHEF HAS COOKED UP FOR YOU UNLESS YOU READ AND STUDY THE MENU.

TRUE: As has been made clear in numerous management books and magazine articles, every organization is unique. Different people with different personalities and idiosyncrasies. Different views, different perceptions. Move into a new organization and to succeed you have to adjust and "fit in".

ALSO TRUE: Every organization is *the same*. Every for-profit company must have the bottom line as a major concern. Every organization must sell: its products, its services, its ideas. It must sell in the field or a store. It must receive and warehouse goods. Manufacture and ship products. Track and safeguard inventories. Establish and support a payables department, credit operation, financial management, advertising and promotion, a research and/or lab operation, personnel, human resources.

Point one is this. Despite organizational uniqueness and differences, *individual skills* are interchangeable. If you can sell razor blades you can also sell furniture. If you can conduct audits and prepare financial statements for a software producer you can do the same thing for a food distributor. If you can create motivational programs for a public utility, you can dream up programs for an engineering firm as well. It might require new approaches, strategies, or techniques, but the basic background, training, and experience will still serve you well.

Point two is that, given the *sameness* of organizations worldwide, it makes no sense to confine your occupational options – money-making or otherwise – to the limited scope of your narrow career and societal experience. Since the marketplace is your oyster, **explore the marketplace!**

I can think of no better example than yours truly. If someone had told me X years ago that I would wind up as a vice president of a university, I would have questioned their sanity. My roots are in manufacturing. But for over a decade that was a thing of the past. Thanks to having broadened my sights to include the whole marketplace, I broadened my career ventures as well which ranged for author-lecturer to radio station operator, hotel owner, and a wide variety of cultural and educational, non-profit enterprises.

Frances Shipley of Fort Lauderdale is another case in point. Executive assistant to an accounting firm's managing director for 22 years, when she was downsized at age 61, she was unable to find employment with another accounting or financial services company. Combing the help wanted columns, and reasoning she had nothing to lose, she responded to an ad that called for secretary to a health care administrator. He liked what he saw, and Shipley liked the deal she was offered. What she can't get over, she says, is how much her previous and new job have in common.

Counseling a young person -- or senior -- in search of employment, I invariably suggest that they use the red pencil technique. It is as simple as it is effective. Armed with a red pencil and the help wanted page, you scroll down the columns and circle any ad at all that in your wildest imagination might be a job you could handle. Obviously, if your training and experience don't fit you would bypass medical, scientific, or technical jobs, for example, that couldn't conceivably apply. But if there's one chance in a hundred, and you have the time on your hands, take a flyer at the job. Arrange for an interview if you can. And take a cue from Fran Shipley's experience. If you're seeking work in the PR or advertising field, for example, don't confine your search to ad agencies or public relations firms. Take a shot at hospitals, educational institutions, utilities, manufacturing companies and distributors, or any other organizations that require promotional services. And keep in mind that every interview you set up will be on the one hand an educational experience, and on the other an opportunity to hone your interviewing skills and techniques.

For Seniors-To-Be With Something To Say

Lucky you. Let's say you have something important to say, idealistic, helpful to others, or cherished memories you want to preserve. Let's say too that you are also fortunate enough to be able devote a chunk of your time to this project without having to worry about financial reward or, unless you're a celebrity with built-in sales success, the dollars you may have to shell out to get what you want to say said.

So, assuming you have something to say and the resources and motivation to get it said, here's another great option to consider. **Write a book.** Or a few articles or Op Ed pieces that set you up as an authority on one subject or other. For example, I've done a series of articles on volunteerism and fostered the payment of "civic rent" concept. Others have picked up on the idea which helped my networking efforts and caused me to become a community presence in both Ohio and Southern Florida.

Book writing is more of an investment. I'll concede that even under the best of circumstances, writing a book is a financial gamble. But if you can afford the crapshoot, the experience can be worthwhile, instructive, exciting and fun.

I recently chatted with friend and fellow author, Ray Dreyfack who helped me with this book, about the pros and cons of book writing in general and penning family histories in particular as an option for seniors on the road to renewal. Dreyfack called to mind an assignment he undertook some years back to record the long-running battle between the Sperry & Hutchinson Co. and supermarket chains A&P, Safeway, et al over the legality of trading stamps. It was a bitter marketplace battle during which one lawyer died in the courtroom. The story was assigned as part of a Random House book called *Great Marketing Decisions That Affect the Lives of Consumers.*

A central character in the book was Ernest Beineke, S&H's founder and long- time CEO, well into his 90's when the project was undertaken. The purpose of the book, his son William Beineke explained to Dreyfack, was to preserve this important segment of the family's rich history which would be otherwise unrecorded when his father passed on.

Okay, now it's you time. In your active years in the marketplace, have you acquired knowledge that might be of practical value to oth-

67

ers and that you would feel good about sharing? Unique strategies or techniques others might apply to advantage? Would it give you a super-charge to see your ideas or ideals in print? In your infinite wisdom, do you think the information is publishable? You won't know for sure unless you investigate. It will cost little or nothing to check it out with a literary agent or editor. That's exactly what I did in deciding to write this, my third book. The level of enthusiasm I received in response served to multiply the motivation that already had moved me to action.

When bandleader-pianist Peter Duchin decided at age 59 to diversify his things-to-do in the years ahead options by writing a memoir, he remarked about *Ghost of a Chance,* "It was just going to be an anecdotal book about things I saw from the bandstand." But when he discussed it with close personal friend Jackie O, she said, "Look, there's a lot more to talk about because your life was so weird and there's been so much tragedy and pain. If you have the guts, do it." Duchin had and he did. In his blockbuster of a book he tells of his experiences and relationships with his famous dad, Eddie, family friend Averill Herriman, and his own wife, herself a best-selling author, producer Leland Hayward, actresses Margaret Sullivan, Kim Novak, Ava Gardner, Aristotle Onassis, to cite a small sampling. What started as a more or less casual undertaking developed into a thrilling experience.

What about you? Looking back over the years, what kind of life did you lead? Dull and ordinary? Or exciting, adventurous, and filled with unusual anecdotes? When your date at heaven's portal arrives, do you want this rich lifetime of memories to peter out with you? (No pun intended.) How would your spouse and kids feel about seeing the family history preserved forever in print? In considering your renewal options, why not take a crack at what for many is the dream of a lifetime – seeing your name on the cover of a book.

I know of no better cure for boredom than diversity. No better prescription for excitement and fulfillment. Comedian Alan King who certainly can afford to rest on his proverbial laurels and take life

68

easy in his 70's and 80's would be appalled at that thought. On the subject of options, King struts out the cliché' of the century: "The more the merrier."

Never the one to turn away from a new challenge or opportunity, he has been in several movies, participated in entrepreneurial ventures from a line of clothing to tennis tournament enterprises. He founded the Alan King Diagnostic Medical Center, established a scholarship fund at Hebrew University in Jerusalem, organized a Laugh Well service which brings entertainers to New York City's sick and elderly, emceed a 25th celebration for the State of Israel at the Citadel of David. And in his "leisure" he took the time to write four books, the latest as of this writing, his autobiography.

Bored? Alan King? Ask him that and he'll give you that famous Alan King shrug. "Who has the time?" Most important, says King, he's doing what he loves to do.

That the true bottom line.

Don't Psyche Yourself or Let Others Psyche You

Some years back, while serving as a vice-president and group executive for American Standard Inc., I wrote an article for *Management Review* titled "How To Conquer the Panic of Change." For too many millions of people the 'panic of change' strikes at a time when they are confronted with the twin shockers of downsizing or forced retirement and the drilled-in mindset that what lies ahead is little more than bleak and solemn "old age". Reinforced by the deeply dug-in cultural misconception that sixty-plus is the end of the road or close to it, it's no surprise that Monster Panic takes over.

In the article I wrote: Analyzing the panic of change, I have found it derives from four separate roots of apprehension:

- First and most important, we possess undefined and often irrational fears based on what we neither know nor understand.

- We lack the self-confidence to assert to ourselves that we have what it takes to come out on top whatever change may take place.

- We're afraid that change may disrupt our comfortable way of life, that a new burden of effort will be foisted on us.

- We are fearful that when change is inflicted upon us, we will in some unknown way be demeaned or disgraced.

In a nutshell we psyche ourselves. Or, just as bad, we let others psyche us. Most significantly, in the order of psychobabble importance: 1. Our kids 2. Other relatives 3. Friends 4. Psychopros.

Our Well-meaning Kids

I find from extensive research that our children are well-meaning in attempting to direct and control our senior years most – but not *all* of – the time. Dual motivations are sometimes in force: 1. Dad's and mom's good health and wellbeing. 2. Ultimate disposition of parents' financial resources.

On occasion the so-called "second time around" can be even more gratifying and fulfilling than the first time around. At least so concluded Susan K. who, at age 63 fell in love – again. Her first husband, Mark, was okay. Susan loved him, she believed. She was a good wife and when Mark failed to survive his third heart attack, she was hit hard by his death and was properly mournful. But life must go on, right? After a respectable period, Susan who is vibrant, sexy, and a great dancer, started dating. When she met Dan, 62, she was almost quite literally, swept off her feet, on the dance floor and off. Fred Astaire had a double. As for Mark, he danced like a *klutz*, had a personality that made Al Gore look exciting, and was a wet dish towel in bed. As for Dan – like Wow! *And he wanted to marry her.*

When her daughters Marsha and Mona and her son Stewart heard the news, their reactions were mixed. Marsh and Stu were devastated, to understate the case. Mona, delighted to see her mother spring out of the doldrums, was delighted. "Hey, Mom," she encouraged, "Go, go, go!"

But the most fervent campaigners were Marsh and Stu. "He's

after your money. Can't you see, Mom, he's after your money."

Susan's financial worth was about $350,000 in cash, mutuals, and her IRA account. "How much is your friend Dan worth, Mom?" She didn't know. Nor did he know *her* net worth. They had never discussed it. "Listen, Mom," Mona said, "don't let this get around, but if there's any truth to Marsh and Stu's charge that he's after your money, I can tell you this: He's not the only one."

Now, after five years of marriage, and still very much in love, Susan says she has never been happier.

Even well-meaning kids can give you a bum steer for the simple reason that nobody knows you like you know yourself. Relying on the advice of family, friends, religious leader, or whoever about critical lifestyle decisions can do you more harm than good because as often or not it is filled with misinformation and misjudgment even if the motivation is high-minded. Advice can be useful as an eye opener, and can present fresh perspectives, just so long as you don't respond with a "must do" mentality.

On the other hand, if plagued by uncertainty, or if you seek reassurance to bolster your own conclusions, soliciting the thoughts of people you trust and respect, can be useful and comforting. But when it comes down to the decision itself, relying more on yourself than anyone else is usually your safest alternative.

Finally, in my experience, in ten cases out of nine, the older you are, the better qualified you will be to make critical life decisions wisely, objectively, and -- sometimes *subjectively* -- with, as in Susan's case, *yourself* as the governing factor.

So many factors are involved -- some unfathomable by others — in determining what is and is not "good for you," it makes no sense to abdicate that responsibility to family, friends, or whoever. Too *old* to decide. Nonsense, unless you've been diagnosed with Alzheimer's or some devastating disease. Millions of Americans, hyped to the hilt about astronaut John Glenn's courage in his venture into space at age 77, never even heard of astronaut trainee Herman Noweck. At 83, Noweck thinks nothing of being strapped into a scary looking contraption that spins him like a gyroscope and simulates all the rigors of space flight. There are some who might call Noweck loco. But if you're his brand of loco you would pay the naysayers no heed. Too old? Don't buy it. When re-**FIRED**, ten times out of nine, if you *think* you can do it, you can.

Don't take my word for it. Check it out with people like venerable White House correspondent Helen Thomas, 78; choreographer Merce Cunningham, 79; jazz musician Billy Taylor, 79; journalist-lecturer-panelist Eric Ober, 86; and Victor Borge at 90 whose performance is enhanced by his clever and charming response when he misses a note here and there. The list could go on and on – and on. So if you're 50 going on 80, this is something to think about.

Be Objective: Is That Other Job Really Better?

"Henry, what's bugging you?" Henry's perceptive wife Jane wanted to know.

"I was bypassed for branch manager again, that's what."

"Hey, you're 63 years old. Come on!"

Antsy, competitive Henry didn't see it that way. "Look at Bill Seeley. Look at Charley Campbell. They don't have half my brains or experience. They got promoted. Why not me?"

"So what are you planning to do?" Jane asked.

"Shop the market. I'm qualified for a manager's job."

"You certainly are," Jane agreed, "but before shopping, take time to check out that manager's job. The pressures and hours involved. Are you ready to saddle yourself with that kind of burden? With your angina?"

Henry wasn't so sure. What Jane said made sense but… The 'but' can be a big one. Henry would be best served with a mindset that applied his valuable management skills to a pursuit he long had wanted to follow without worrying about status and focusing on simply "doing his thing."

Some people are never satisfied with what they have and who they are. It's part of their nature. The status quo isn't good enough. That's well and good for someone who could and should be doing better. But for many the status quo is as good as it gets, sometimes *better* than it might get if you mess around with it. Take show business great Bob Hope, actor, entertainer, comedian. Opportunities were coming out of the woodwork. He brushed them aside. Successful, satisfied, and effective all his life, the status quo was good enough for him. Henry made a wise choice in deciding not to rock the boat.

We're creatures of habit. Set on comparing ourselves with others. Associates, relatives, friends. How am I doing compared to Frank, Harry, and Joe? Who cares? Who really cares? It's fine to compete, but don't compete against yourself. In considering your options, bring them into perspective.

Zero In On Tomorrow

Someone once said, "Keep your eye on the future, because that's where you'll spend the rest of your life," or words to that effect.

It's a thought to take with you when you consider your options. It is hard to stop your mind from dwelling on actions and decisions you made in the past. But I find it important to do so. The past is the past...let it rest in peace. Keep your eye on the future.

74

Chapter 5

Flourish Amidst the New Realities

Cash In On Your Edge

"To be happy we must face reality"

Maxwell Maltz

How often when you were a kid of 5, 6, or 8 did you confront your mother with the lament, almost an accusation at times: "Mommy, I'm bored."

At those times, how did your mother respond? If typical, she probably said, "Go out and play." Or, "Work on your coloring book." Or, "Play with your building blocks." Or, "Clean up your room."

From your perspective at the time, her *ideal* response would have been to find something interesting for you to do, something you really wanted to do. Or better still, to stop what she was doing, set aside the vacuum, stop her ironing, or whatever, and devote her attention to you. Perhaps on occasion that's what she did do. But most often it just wasn't practical. Mommy had her own needs and responsibilities to worry about.

Isn't it ironic that for so many people life's cycle seems to spin around all the way back to START so that after leaving the workplace, voluntarily or not, they find themselves plagued by the same sad lament, articulated or not? Boredom is a deadly deteriorator. Golf doesn't suffice. Leisure palls. A person can read or travel just so much. The time vacuum has to be filled.

With what? Mommy's no longer at hand or, if she is, she's in no position to find interesting activities for you to pursue. The only one who can do that is *you*.

As I stress in this book, the ideal time to address this universal mind-boggling dilemma is in one's 50's or earlier. But the good news is that it's never too late just so long as you're mentally conditioned to face up to the challenge. The important thing is not so much where we stand now as where we are headed.

Spell Out Your Objectives

Let's hypothesize. You are 55 or 60, in reasonably good health. What do you want your life to be like when you hit 65 or 70?

Maybe you like your job or the business you're running. If so, do you want the status quo to persist? You probably do, at least for a while. But – remember, we're hypothesizing – do you want to keep on devoting 8 or 10 hours a day to the job? Before you answer too fast, take a moment or two to reflect. What about all those *other things* you always wanted to do, but kept putting off: Becoming better acquainted with your kids and grandchildren; seeing some more of the world; contributing a little payback to the community that treated you so well; developing that maybe not so wild idea that's been germinating in back of your mind; giving your spouse a break with his or her desires in mind; getting around to some of those books you've been meaning to read, or write; yes, even spending more time on the golf links or tennis court?

Or maybe you've "had it" with your business or the job you've been crunching for years. In that case, all the more reason to ponder the future life changes you would like to make. So, the big question is: Where do you go from here?

STEP ONE IS TO DEVELOP A CAREFULLY
PLANNED GOAL-DIRECTED MINDSET!!!

Project ahead to five or ten years down the road. Construct a mental picture of the lifestyle scenario you would most like to see materialize. Make a list of the activities – income-based and otherwise – you would most like to pursue. Realistically, practically, and unselfishly, bring your loved ones into the act. But it's *your* life, so remember that you're in charge, the final decisions yours to make.

Take your list and prioritize it. On the one hand, be realistic and practical; on the other, give your imagination full rein. Then begin setting goals for yourself and, most important of all, don't permit distractions, subterfuges, and influences allow your goals to disappear into thin air. As English author Hannah More wrote: "Obstacles are those frightful things you see when you take your eyes off the goal."

Finally, take a cue from the professional success merchandisers. Strongly objective-focused, they advise: If you really want to succeed at whatever goal you set for yourself, keep the *reward* in your mind's eye as you shoot for the goal. Salespeople in a sales-building contest, for example, are advised to keep concentrating on that Hawaiian vacation for two, or that sleek automobile, in competing to win.

You can do the same thing. Visualize your new freedom from stress; the joys of finally getting to know your grandchildren; renewed love and romance with your spouse; the spiritual rewards of community service; the time you will have when your goal is achieved to travel, socialize, and have fun.

Time, in the final reckoning, is what this is all about.

Get Rid of the Garbage

"Did you take the garbage out, dear?"

I couldn't tell you how many times Phyllis has posed this question to me over the past three or four decades. But one day recently the question triggered a thought. How many of us 'take out the garbage' on a day to day basis, but fail to take the garbage out of our lives? Well, the older and more savvy we become, the more adept we are – or should be – at taking the garbage out of our lives.

"60 Minutes'" Steve Kroft spelled this out clearly in a 90-minute documentary on "60 Minutes" creator, hard-nosed, scrappy Don Hewitt who, at age 45, first logged the CBS program 30+ years ago. As the documentary makes clear, Hewitt is still going strong at age 77.

In the film, titled "90 Minutes on '60 Minutes," Kroft explained why Hewitt states, "I don't feel any older now than I did when I started the broadcast." His secret? He developed a "taking out the garbage" mindset that excludes from his things-to-do menu tasks he does not want to do, what I refer to as occupational garbage. High up on his list are such items as "budgetary matters" which Hewitt makes it a point to ignore.

The concept isn't new. Smart executives apply it all the time under a different label. It is called *delegation.* It's a thought to take with you. How many distasteful tasks, or chores beneath your level of compensation or competence, can you pass on to others, subordinates, your kids, your spouse, whoever. Delegation needn't be confined to the workplace. The more skillfully you can collect the garbage in your life and have it carted off by others, the more effectively you will overcome boredom and make your life more interesting and productive.

Stay Busy, But Not Too Busy

A philosopher whose name escapes me referred to time as "the raw material of life." The trick is to master time without permitting time to master you. The ideal is to keep active and productive without overdoing it. On the one hand, no asset I can think of is more precious than time. On the other, nothing I know appears to get browbeaten more ruthlessly and persistently than the clock.

It's no secret that pressure can be good or bad. A reasonable amount of pressure adds dynamism and excitement to every endeavor, helps the adrenaline flow. If for years you have been active and under pressure in your job or business, the sudden disappearance of pressure when downsized or retired can be devastating. It is a factor that is rarely discussed or considered. A total absence of pressure in my experience is a harbinger of boredom.

Paul G., an executive I know was for years a controller for a medium sized food products distributor. His company, on a cost-cutting binge, at age 54, his assistant was upgraded and Paul was downsized. Totally unexpected, he was stunned. Close to tears, Paul confided in language not fit to print, how he felt and the havoc this played on his id. For as long as he could remember his days and decisions had been ruled by the clock. Phone calls, conferences, lunch meetings, sudden trips, problems to solve, fires to put out. Pressure's gift had been a developing ulcer. But now that it was gone his rhythm system was messed up.

"It's like I'm suddenly *empty*." An appropriately descriptive word.

I asked, "Did you ever plan for this eventuality?"

He shook his head. "Who knew? I never dreamed..." He and the president had always had good rapport.

Wanting to comfort him, I tried to convince him it wasn't too late.

He couldn't see it, didn't buy it, at least not at the time. But finally we started to discuss his situation. I fired a barrage of questions at him. Asset reserves? Better than comfortable. Job satisfaction? Meager. Health? Blood pressure too high. Family relationship? Testy.

"So, if you had your druthers, Paul, where would you want to go from here?"

That was four years ago. Today, Paul is a manufacturer's rep in the industry he knows so well, earning 70 percent of his former income, more than enough to get by on. His former employer is his best account. Paul has never felt so healthy. He no longer needs Viagra.

Work-weary? Think Twice.

What would life be without meaningful work?

Ponder this typical scenario. The guy is fully employed. His wife loves him. He does his thing; she does hers.. Then suddenly, deciding he feels "beat", he opts for early retirement -- Ugh, that word again! -- with no plan in mind other than to spend more time with his children and grand kids, have more time for reading, travel, and golf.

Scott C., a well heeled Ohio plant executive, was custom built to that model. When he opted for early retirement at age 60 his belief that he had made a smart decision persisted for about four months. The six-week vacation he and Mae had long talked about taking was fun. The occasional trips to visit his widespread kids and grand children were indulgences he had rarely had time for on the job. But as the weeks dragged by after and he and Mae "settled down," Scott found himself with 'Time on His Hands'. When Ray Noble recorded that song, he must have had Scott in mind.

The golf he had enjoyed when it was a weekend privilege suddenly lost its appeal. He could have afforded more vacations but had somehow lost the urge. Besides which, Mae had her clubs, community service activities, and bridge games. Scott as a home body was messing up her routine. As for him, he spent more and more time lounging around, napping before the TV – driving Mae out of her skull.

He never actually said, "Mommy, I'm bored", but savvy Mae got the message. Another thing Scott didn't articulate was how much he missed the job where he had been important, productive. He kept berating himself. Dumbest thing I ever did, opting for early retirement. Smart cookie, Mae. She called an old friend and explained the predicament.

"Ellie, is Ted still putting in three days a week on that job he got when he was downsized?"

"Oh, sure. He loves it." Ted was a longtime associate of Scott's; they had worked together for years.

"Do you think there might be room in his company for someone like Scott?"

"I don't know; let me check."

You can probably guess the rest of the story. The lesson is

clear. Thousands, perhaps *millions* of people, hitting on 60 or older, decide that they've "had it" with their jobs when, what they've actually had it with are the long hours and excess pressure that left them little time for other pursuits. The answer for many, like Scott, may be not to quit or accept retirement, but to taper down, often these days a very do-able option.

Mae's problem, that of the spouse suddenly saddled with a husband who for years went to work every day and all at once finds himself house bound with time to kill, is by no means uncommon. Typically, wives of active men like Scott, are themselves dynamic and busy with club, social, and community activities occupying much of their time.

My dear wife Phyllis, as well as anyone I know, conforms to this pattern. Productively busy, the days aren't long enough. The family things we enjoy together are mostly in the evenings and weekends. The last thing Phyllis would need is for me to be messing up her time commitments with my irresistible presence around the house. Or as Phyllis states the case: "I married for love, not for lunch."

How Realistic Is the Taper-Down Alternative?

How realistic? Whatever your age, it depends most of all, first, on how you feel about how you are investing the most precious asset you will ever have, *your time;* and second, on what you would *rather* be doing, for at least some of that time.

Some people derive so much pleasure and satisfaction from their work that, as Lila C. states the case, "I'll never quit so long as I am physically and creatively capable of doing it."

Lila, widowed at age 56, does fancy embroideries, some of which she sells, others of which she gifts to friends, neighbors, and relatives and uses to decorate her home. She says, "I enjoy an occasional game of bridge, and help out at a senior center nearby. But whatever I do, it's fun to get back to my embroidery."

Total dedication to a cause or career is a blessing second to none. I think it was Renoir who was so passionate regarding his painting that when, so crippled by arthritis he could no longer hold a brush in his hands, he clenched the brush between his teeth and continued to paint?

Quit working? "I've been doing it for 43 years, and I'm not about to stop now," declares octogenarian Abigail Van Buren, whose Dear Abby column is enjoyed by 90 million readers worldwide. Assisted by a staff of six who sort the 1,000 to 5,000 letters she gets weekly, Van Buren puts in at least eight hours each day.

Quit working? No way! Famed comedy writer Larry Gelbart, 71, whose clients ran from Bob Hope, Jack Benny, and Sid Caeser to Danny Kaye, Art Carney and Eddie Cantor, is equally adamant. He has been making audiences laugh for 56 years as his reruns from 'Lucy', M*A*S*H', and other shows affirm. As Van Buren puts it, he's not about to stop now. Why should he? He's having a ball.

Admittedly, individuals who are so blessed as to love their careers with a passion are in the minority. Most people, as they approach their 60's and 70's, don't want to 'throw in the sponge', but ideally, would prefer cutting their work time 20 to 50 percent. Well, the good news is that never before in my memory has the economic climate been better suited to accommodate this preference.

IF YOU HAVE A SKILL, TALENT, OR SPECIALIZED KNOWLEDGE OF SOME KIND, THESE DAYS YOU ARE A MUCH SOUGHT AFTER COMMODITY. ALL YOU NEED TO DO IS GET FOUND.

Your working experience is worth a mint if you cash in on it. Employers nationwide cite recruitment of skilled people as a major objective and one of the most difficult to meet. An equally important goal, and one that goes hand in hand with recruitment, is in this era of raging downsizing and turnover, the task of retaining existing employees and keeping them nose-grounded to the grindstone.

No better example could be found than the field of accounting. A battle royal, reports *The Wall Street Journal* writer Sue

Shallenbarger, is under way among the so-called Big Six accounting giants to get on best-employer lists with "a blizzard of new initiatives, from flexible schedules to novel career tracks." As the skilled-labor market tightens, she goes on to say, "similar rivalries may heat up (not may heat up, but are heating up) in other fields. Meanwhile, the Battle of the Big Six has created a crucible for work innovation." Plus unprecedented opportunities.

The Short Workday Solution

A boon for the new tapered down generation, the abbreviated workday is no less a boon for a growing number of employers. A human resources executive who prefers to remain unidentified, says, "A year or so ago, with turnover excessive, we were desperate for experienced office and plant personnel. At a high level meeting we came to the conclusion that we had to redefine the word "old." And we had to redefine the workday as well."

In the past this company, sensitive to age discrimination laws, didn't out-and-out reject job applicants past fifty, but as the executive puts it, "We were culturally brainwashed to favor people in their 30's and 40's. Nor had we given much thought to alternatives to the 40-hour work week."

In response, the company made radical changes in its personnel policies and procedures. A training program was initiated to achieve the following new mindsets among supervisors, managers, human resources and personnel employees:

- Department heads were encouraged to ignore age – not only figuratively, but psychologically -- in hiring and promoting employees.

- Existing and new employees were permitted to "negotiate" alternative work weeks with supervisors – shorter hours on the one hand, flex time arrangements on the other.
- The key criteria sought in hiring people were experience, credentials, and work record with previous employers.

Results were more than gratifying, my informant reports after the program was in force six months. Employee turnover dropped 13% over the same six months of the previous year. Recruitment efforts improved an estimated 18%. The executive adds, "We now have 16 percent of the workforce on a flex time or curtailed workweek arrangement, half composed of younger people who opted for change due to 'family convenience,' most of the rest are employees over 50 or 60."

Smart Options

Knowledgeable employers in today's market know that smart options aren't necessarily the ones you call your broker about. For an increasing number of savvy managers and supervisors, retention of valuable people boils down to a choice of workplace options the employee can live with.

CASE IN POINT NO. 1 – Martha J. (age 56)

Martha, a talented and experienced window dresser employed by a successful women's wear shop, was torn between two realities of her working life. A widow, she loved what she was doing and didn't want to give it up. But her full time job conflicted with her family responsibilities, most specifically caring for a mother who suffered from Alzheimer's disease. Her sister helped, but the burden on her was unfair.

If you love what you do, why quit? But sometimes you can't help yourself. Unless… Martha decided to cash in on her edge – years of experience and unmatched savvy. She approached her boss and leveled with him. "I'd hate to resign, but I may have no choice."

Frowning, the surprised manager asked, "What's the problem?"

"Time," Martha replied. "If we could work out an arrangement where I would work three days a week instead of five…"

Her boss looked thoughtful for no more than two seconds. "You got it," he replied.

CASE IN POINT NO. 2 – Steve M. (age 66)

Financial vice president of a plumbing supplies company, Steve was in much the same boat as Martha. He's good at what he does and doesn't want to stop doing it. But his wife Ann finally put down her foot. Enough is enough! Steve and Ann both enjoy golf. They love visiting their grandkids when and if they can get around to it. They appreciate cultural and recreational pursuits on the rare occasions Steve finds time to pursue them. And they've been planning a vacation to Greece for years. What Steve could really use are some 36-hour days.

But reality is reality. High level jobs like Steve's are demanding with long hours and little time for golf, travel, or grandkids. So what to do? Quit? He might have to, Steve reasoned, unless...

Steve knew of others who had done it, why not him? It might be a long shot, but it was worth a try. Steve talked to his boss, the company's CEO. He proposed a voluntary cut in his 6-figure income in exchange for a license to come and go as he pleased. What about all his work and obligations? No problem, Steve assured the chief. He would continue to handle the sensitive high priority stuff, train subordinates to take on the rest, delegate lesser tasks and oversee their performance. This should chop his hours in half. His boss thought it over and decided Steve was too valuable to lose.

Stories like these abound in the workplace. Experience is your working capital. To cash in on it all it takes is a bit of imagination, and the courage and smarts to seek new and different alternatives.

The Golden Gap

If you're in your 40's or 50's you're lucky. You still have the Golden Gap to look forward to. The Gap as I define it is the period of one's life from the mid-fifties to the eighties and beyond during which millions of intelligent and thoughtful people really and truly mature, become more knowledgeable, more skilled, more sensitive, more compassionate, better human beings in general.

I consider myself fortunate that as of this writing I am continuing to cash in on my Golden Gap enrichment. When I think of all the dumb things and half-assed decisions I made in my earlier years that by no stretch of the imagination I would do today, it is mind-boggling. I could write a book on that subject alone. I'd be willing to bet that an untold number of people in their 60's, 70's, and 80's, would vehemently echo this sentiment. The reality is that ten, fifteen, twenty years ago I would not have been *qualified* to accomplish what I am doing today. So what is all this crap about being too old? **Too old for what?**

The point is if you are really good you are *needed* – whatever your age. By your boss, by your company, by the men and women who directly or indirectly enjoy and appreciate the work you produce. Venerable United Press correspondent Helen Thomas, 78, still covers the White House daily. The job she does won her millions of readers and fans and innumerable awards over the years. Is her age a hindrance? Anything but! Thomas is smarter and more experienced today than she was ten years ago at age 68. Successful in her 40's, a book could be written on the savvy and smarts she acquired since that time. Friends and family sometimes urge her to retire and take life easy. The journalist's response: "I'll quit when I stop having fun."

Practice Practical Past Life Progression

The time, 5 years ago. Magda X, age 41, single, height 5'5, weight 181 lbs., had a problem. You guessed it – sadly overweight. A compulsive eater, actually, Magda has a pretty face, but the excess lard had for years plagued her life and her lifestyle. After all, not many normal red-blooded men are willing to date severely overweight women. So what to do? Magda had lost count of the number of diets she had started and broke, the amount of resolutions that fizzled. Friends didn't help, therapists didn't help, Mom's entreaties didn't help.

One day a doctor friend told Magda, "Maybe, if you could find out why you can't seem to help stuffing yourself, you could stop doing it." The physician suggested she see a psychiatrist. Desperate, as a last resort, Magda agreed.

The doctor interviewed her and suggested she try past life therapy. "What's that?"

"Under hypnosis, I scroll you back in time to earlier years of your life. In effect you will relive past life experiences. If we're lucky we may hit on something that happened that subconsciously triggered your over-eating compulsion."

It didn't sound too hopeful to Magda, but she reasoned, What do I have to lose?

Magda lucked out. Regression showed that as a teenager in Czechoslovakia her father had been killed in an accident and her family had come on hard times. In those days Magda was *always* hungry. In time her mother's brother sponsored their relocation to America, and the family's economic situation improved. But as the doctor explained, the hunger period had become impressed deep down in Magda's self-conscious and had triggered her over-eating compulsion. Once this was explained, doctor and patient worked together to overcome the problem.

Over several months Magda was able to shed 46 pounds. Today she is dating.

The good news is that 'practical past life' progression need not be this formal, complicated, or expensive, to help achieve your renewal goal. And it needn't require hypnosis. It can be a do-it-yourself proposition. Pondering my own life experience I have found that what I am, what I do, and how I make decisions today are largely the result of what I was, what I did, and how I made decisions in the past, from the time of my childhood to now. What applies to me applies to everyone else.

With this thought in mind I believe you will find it useful to *objectively* and *critically* review the smart and dumb things you have done – at least throughout your working life – with a determination to learn what you can from your experience. We all have successes and failures to recount. Victories and defeats. Smart actions and decisions that moved us ahead towards the fulfillment of our goals. Stupid mistakes that made us fall on our faces.

Think of blunders as learning experiences and even from your goofs you can derive positive value. For example, having owned three hotels in south Florida – two Holiday Inns and one Sheraton – I went belly-up in that enterprise because I was inadequately financed. Needless to say, I would never again go into the hotel business, or any business, without adequate financing. I could point to other blunders as well, some too embarrassing to mention. But I can tell you this: Without mistakes their would not be endeavors.

As experience proves, often failing to make a decision or take an action for fear of being mistaken, can be the biggest mistake of all. Plutarch said almost two thousand years ago: "To make no mistakes is not in the power of man, but from their errors and mistakes the wise and good learn wisdom for the future." The dumbest mistake of all is the one from which you don't learn.

What has this to do with practical past life regression? A good deal. Many people advise, "The past is done, forget about it." I would edit this counsel to read, The past is done, don't worry about it. But *forgetting* about it could diminish your opportunities to learn. In my experience, reviewing the past can be educational and helpful in planning the future.

So my advice is to roll back the years of your life and call to mind as many meaningful actions and decisions as you can – <u>or actions and decisions you failed to face up to</u> – and jot them down on a sheet of paper or on as many sheets as it takes. Include things you *wanted* to do, but for one reason or other failed to do. Alongside each entry write a brief critical and objective evaluation. Was it smart or dumb? Was it beneficial, or did you lose out in some way? What, specifically, did you do right or wrong? If the same action or decision faced you today, what if anything would you do differently? Finally, take another sheet of paper and, running down your compilation, note what you learned that might influence actions or decisions you might consider with the future in mind. Zero in on things you long have *wanted* to do, but due to circumstances, apprehension, family pressures, or whatever, you neglected to do. If you can fulfill just one longtime dream from this experiment, you will find the time and effort worthwhile. And if nothing else it will pinpoint your strengths and weaknesses.

The purpose of conscious – as opposed to Magda's subconscious regression – is not to relive or bemoan your experience, but to cash in on it with re-**FIRE**-ment in mind.

What If?

What if you had done this or that five, ten, twenty years ago? How would it affect what you are doing and your lifestyle today? Forget about those shares of Microsoft or Amacom you might have bought before the stock price went through the ceiling. What-iffing from a rekindlement standpoint, can be a useful exercise if you keep it practical and realistic with achievable goals in mind. Achievable goals! That's the key.

When the Key Doesn't Fit the Lock

We'll talk about the entrepreneurial option in the next chapter, but for now let's assess it from a What if? point of view. A guy I know – he wouldn't want his name revealed, so I'll call him Charley K – is an avid hunter who loves guns. His career as a technologist employed by an industrial tool manufacturer had long since begun to bore him. Every vacation he got Charley he was out in the woods with a buddy or two hunting grouse, deer, or whatever. What if, he mused, I could come up with a career where I could work with guns instead of tools?

Charley opted for "early retirement" at age 55 to pursue a lifelong dream to open a gun shop. Nothing wrong that that, right? I'll have to agree that lifelong dreams are meant to be pursued. Unless... Unless the pursuer is Charley-minded. In Charley's case the key didn't fit the lock. For one thing, he knew nothing about running a business. He never had to meet a payroll or production schedule, he never hired people, he never dealt directly with customers, and it never occurred to him that he would have to put in even longer hours than he had on his job if he wanted to make it

89

work. On top of that, in failing to analyze what he had going for him, and what obstacles he might run into, he neglected to anticipate his wife's response to his entrepreneurial aspirations. Fortunately, when Mabel laid it on the line ("It's either me or that damn gun shop!"), Charley gave up the store.

Shallow-minded planning is the negative part of the what-if approach to refiring and renewing your life. You either do it realistically, or flounder.

When the key does fit, however, it can be a beautiful experience, especially if you approach it with eclectically selected role models in mind. How do you *really* want to spend the rest of your life. What would you most like to do? Don't limit yourself or be too specific.

Unless you already have an absolutely positive answer to these questions in mind, it might help to tear another sheet of paper from that pad and list a handful of people in your acquaintance whom you truly admire and would most like to emulate. Alongside each name enter *why* you hold them in such high esteem. Is it because of what they have, how they act, the activities they engage in, or what – apart from material possessions – they have achieved? Then calculate as objectively and realistically as possible exactly what steps you would need to take to put yourself in their shoes. Armed with this information, your renewal goals should be easy to set.

Chapter 6

Should You Run Your Own Show?

Starting and Building a Business

"Work as if you were to live 100 years.
Pray as if you were to die tomorrow."

Benjamin Franklin

Basically, in the marketplace, there are two kinds of people: 1. Movers and builders. 2. Grunts. Movers work hard to further their goal of personal growth and development. The grunts man the trenches, work their butts off to scrape by.

How do you rate yourself? If you're a dyed in the wool grunt, it could require a massive effort to avoid the moribund morass of (oh, hated word!) retirement. For movers in their 50's, 60's, and 70's, contemplating their what-lies-ahead lifestyle, it's a different story entirely. Ann Richards, former Texas governor and now a lobbyist and women's causes activist, puts it neatly: "I can't figure out what I would do if I didn't work."

Eleanor Roosevelt, a tireless worker for social advancement during FDR's presidency, like Richards, couldn't imagine a life of idleness. She had her own radio program, and wrote a nationally syndicated newspaper column, "My Day", along with various crusades of one kind of other. At her husband's death friends and family urged her to settle down at last and become a proper grandma.

She pondered this a minute or so, and even more briefly, when invited to become a U.S. delegate to the United Nations. Was she psychologically ready at age 61 for a major career change? Indeed she was! Ready enough to help draft the UN Declaration of Human Rights, and in her spare time write a couple of books, "This I Remember" in 1949, and her autobiography in 1961.

So the choice facing you is clear: Retirement, or firing up a new life. Some people have grown to believe that retirement is a right; I contend it's a wrong. For one thing, opting for early retirement instead of the gutsy renewal approach is bad for the economy as it is for you. Investment banker and chairman of the Institute for International Economics, Peter G. Peterson, states the case bluntly enough in his book, "How the Coming Age Wave Will Transform America – and the World" (Times Books 1999): "Early retirement is already undermining the survival of developed nations." In Singapore, the government is trying to boost the retirement age from 62 to 67.

The Guttsiest Way to Refuel and Renew.

It's not for everyone. The aim here is to determine, after careful investigation and planning, if going into – or staying in -- business for yourself is for you. It's no secret to anyone that most new enterprises don't make it. The trick is to find out for yourself *in advance* what your chances of success or failure may be.

One thing I've learned from hard, and at times bitter experience, is that success doesn't happen automatically. *You have to plan for it to happen!* Most people fail to do this so they flop. Most often, their capitalization planning is flawed. Joe, Harry, or Marge gets this or that great inspiration to open a gas station, tour guide service, or dress shop. They talk to friends, neighbors, or family members who are all gung ho for the idea, and in they plunge. All of a sudden they realize they'll need another $75,000 to support or expand the enterprise, and when the bank says no, it goes rapidly downhill.

Don't Endow Friends with Expertise

Friends mean well. But that doesn't make them experts. To plan a business properly you need a carload of information. Market information. Financial information. Competitive information. Pricing information. Legal information. Time commitment information. Facts and projections that could make guesswork suicidal. If I had a dollar for every piece of wrong information provided would-be entrepreneurs by well meaning friends or family members, I'd probably edge out Bill Gates as the richest man in the world.

The information is there for the taking, but you have to dig it out, and sometimes you have to pay for it. If you need financial information, consult a banker and make sure the commercial ax he has to grind doesn't color his advice. The trick is to search for, not only expert but objective, opinions. Experts on virtually every phase of business enterprise are available, sometimes for free, sometimes for a price. If the capital investment is sizable, it makes sense to confirm one guru's opinion with that of another.

One further tip. Before investing a bundle on expert advice, spend some time on the internet, or ask a computer buff to help you do it if your internet savvy is lacking. Many public library staffers are only too willing to link you up with business and senior web sites and chat groups pregnant with all kinds of information and advice on what the fledgling entrepreneur needs and what pitfalls to avoid.

Thinking of buying a business? Florida *Sun-Sentinel* columnist Richard Hodgetts suggests 5 critical questions to ask: 1. Why is the business being sold? 2. What is the physical condition of the business? 3. How many key personnel will be staying? 4. What does the competition look like? 5. Will the seller agree not to compete?

Keep Your Boss's Objectives In Mind

So you plan to own a business and think you're the boss. Think again. No way are you the boss! Your *customers* are in charge if you're smart and lucky enough to get them. In my experience, more businesses go belly up because of poor, negligent, and just plain *dumb* customer service than for any other reason. A few years back I conducted a survey to determine how guests felt about the service offered by various South Florida hotels. Roughly half the respondents said the service they received was either downright awful, poor, or at best only fair.

Customer service, like any other function of business, doesn't just happen. You have to plan to make it happen, and then check regularly to be sure your plan is being adhered to. Stressing superior customer service is one of the surest, and most cost-effective ways of ensuring business success. If you are not in a position to exceed or, at the very least equal, the service of your closest competitors, you would be best advised to seek another rekindlement option.

Just Keep On Doing What You're Doing

The preferred way to run your own show whether you're 40, 60, or 70 is when capitalization is no problem and you don't need to consult any experts for advice on the financial aspects of going into business. Edmund Aleks, retired from the Los Angeles District Attorney's office at age 55 and is well into his second career running his own investigative service. Jack A. Berman, 84, has reduced his work hours, reports *New York Times* writer Jan. M. Rosen, but enjoys an activity-filled life. A former business professor at the Chicago campus of Northwestern University, he has never stopped teaching. Berman prefers the word transition to retirement, although New Age enthusiasts might question that choice. He has a friend, he says, who retired as a physician but, having also been a musician, organized a chamber orchestra. Stories like this abound. Examples:

Cal Clinton – At age 52, the Fort Lauderdale public relations executive decided it was time to play *Switch*. The decision, based on well planned and analyzed factors, was one neither Cal nor his banker and professional friends, could knock any holes into. The plan was to make boating and fishing , his long-loved hobby and recreational pursuit, his new occupation, and PR on a freelance basis his avocation if need be,. Cal's charter boat service took off from the start. With his income rising each month, there has been no need to freelance.

Dom Ferraro – Dom, a talented landscaping specialist, has had it with his boss who is always on his back. "Hey, Dom, the quicker you finish, the more lawns you cover, the more bread rolls in."

Dom doesn't agree. Any kid can mow a lawn, he argues. It takes service and quality to make it as a landscaping expert. Dom works fast, but takes pains with trimming and pruning, discusses ideas with his customers. His eye for beauty demands excellence. His boss on the other hand mixes cheap seed with the good seed he charges to customers. He calls this smart. Dom calls it cheating.

"I can't take it any more," he tells his wife Angie. "I wanna start my own business." Angie doesn't reply. But she's worried.

At 53 should Dom take the plunge? Give up a regular paycheck? Face the insecurity? Actually, no big investment was involved. He already owned a station wagon and most of the equipment required. And, having earned a reputation for honest and superior quality, when he made the change referrals came pouring in.

Alyson Ringer – Alyson, 50, was in pretty much the same boat. With 15 years' experience as secretary to a real estate executive and salesperson in the field, should she resign and set out on her own. Her dad, a semi-retired insurance agent, helped her form her rationale. "Why not, Al, you've got the needed know-how and experience; your income needs aren't that great; you want more time to spend with the kids; and you can work from an office at home. No more than a minimal investment is needed. The risk isn't all that great. If it doesn't work out, any real estate office in town would grab you up in a flash. Take a shot at it." She did. That was three years ago and she's still shooting.

MORAL OF THESE STORIES:
WHEN YOU KNOW YOUR FIELD AND INCOME REQUIRE-
MENTS, HAVE NO WORRIESOME FINANCIAL INVEST-
MENT AT RISK, HAVE A STRONG CUSTOMER BASE FROM
WHICH TO WORK, AND HAVE THE GUTS TO STRIKE
OUT ON YOUR OWN, YOUR CHANCE FOR SUCCESS
WILL BE MULTIPLIED.

Are You Ready?

Operating your own business can be a wonderful life-renewing experience – especially if you've never done it before. But if you take the jump prematurely, it can turn into a total disaster. Adequate preparation implies readiness on all fronts:

- Psychological.
- Physical.
- Financial.
- Sociological.

Many people, middle-aged or older, who decide to run their own show as a rekindlement option, focus heavily on the financial aspects, but shallowly on the other factors which can be equally, and in some cases, more important.

Consider the following questions:

With the rest of your life in mind, how do you want to spend your time?

Boiled down to its essence, your time is your life. The reality of starting your own business is that if your situation is typical, you will be required to spend a great deal more time and effort in getting the enterprise off the ground than you ever dreamed possible. This could mean less time to spend with the family, less time for social and recreational pursuits, less time for travel and cultural activities for months or years at least. Unless your circumstances are atypical, are you ready and willing to make this sacrifice?

Is your health sufficiently strong to hold up under the stress and strain of launching a new enterprise?

Running your own show, as too many have learned the hard way, can take a whole lot out of you. Mike Medlock, a former children's garments sales rep, is still alive the last I heard, possibly thanks to his wife Ann. At age 60 he invested a chunk of money in an on-line enterprise fraught with all kinds of problems. His mental as well as his physical wellbeing started to deteriorate. After he suffered a mini heart attack, and considerable arm twisting on Ann's part, Mike agreed to swallow his losses and give up the ghost on his enterprise. He is now a manufacturer's rep on a part time basis and enjoying good health again. In lining up your "consultants," a frank talk with your family doctor could well be an item near the top of your list.

Are you willing to cut back on the travel, socializing, and fun and games you've enjoyed for so long – at least for a while if not longer?

Once you run your own show, your time is your own to spend as you see fit? Right? Wrong! Once again, if your situation is typical, when you run your own show, at least at the outset, your time is your business's. In launching an enterprise, rarely if ever, does the time commitment work out as anticipated. Unforeseen problems erupt. New ideas develop that you want to see implemented. Unexpected customer needs occur that can't be postponed if you want the business to succeed. Again, while the rewards of successful enterprise can be heady, the piper must be paid in terms of long hours and often unanticipated weekend work.

Is the financial investment realistic?

The answer to this question depends on the kind of business you have in mind. Some enterprises can be started on a proverbial shoestring or less. Others require a chunk of money. Can you work the operation from your home? Will office space be needed? Production tools and machinery? One or more computers? What about personnel? Will this be a one-man operation? Or will you need salespeople, a secretary, office help? What will your staffing costs be? Will you need an accountant, a lawyer? How much will you have to pay for financial advice?

How does your family tie into this venture?

Are your spouse and children solidly supportive of the venture? Do you plan to have your spouse or children participate in any way? This could be the most important question of all. When I went into the hotel business my wife Phyllis's involvement was crucial to the success of the enterprise. She functioned as executive vice president. Her commitment to customer service was no less wholehearted than my own. She selected the staff uniforms and made sure they fit. She spot-checked room-service trays as they left the kitchen. Is there enough butter? Is the coffee steaming hot? Will a guest have to call down for mustard or ketchup that should have been sent up but wasn't. Details! Details can make or a break a new enterprise. Phyllis set up and was responsible for décor throughout the hotels. When problems developed we discussed and resolved them together. The critical point is that she *cared* as I myself cared. Too many new businesses are broken on the back of indifference. People close to you care. Others often don't give a damn. Have you considered this factor?

Plan for a Sensible Life Balance

Retirement vs. rekindlement notwithstanding, in planning the rest of your life, like it or not, it makes sense to consider your age as a factor if you contemplate launching a new enterprise. Time commitment is the key. How much time do you *want* to spend on this, that, and the other thing? Will the operation you have in mind be compatible with your hopes and expectations? Will the dog wag the tail, or will the tail wag the dog? Some businesses require a heavy time commitment to succeed. In one's 40's and early 50's you might be willing to make this sacrifice to reap rewards later on.

In your late 50's, 60's and 70's it could be another story entirely. If this is your time frame, what might make the most sense is to opt for a business that can be operated successfully and productively on a part time basis. Some examples:

<u>Accountant</u> – Whether your plan is to specialize in tax work or not, you would be free to limit the number of clients served. You may be able to set up an office and require clients to come to you. An accountant I know has leased commercial space in the large high rise development where she lives. She has a long list of people and small business owners who want her to handle their accounts, and is free to accept or reject clients at will. "The only clients I visit," she says, "are the ones in my own building."

<u>Freelance Writer</u> – A writer I know, now 65, and formerly employed by a New York City public relations agency, decided upon rekindlement that he wanted to limit his working hours to about twenty per week. No problem. He accepts or rejects assignments with this time frame in mind. Happily, last year's rekindlement income exceeded his prior year's full time earnings.

<u>Auto Mechanic</u> – Tony, 53, can take apart an engine and put it together again in less time than it would take most mechanics to evaluate the problem. As much as he loves his work, he readily admits, "I'm basically a lazy person." With his children grown and no longer his responsibility, and with a comfortable nest egg for his wife Marie and himself, he decided he would work when "he felt like it." If you approach him in the right way he will trouble shoot and repair your vehicle; otherwise he'll refuse. Tony's work time commitment ranges from ten to thirty hours per week depending on his mood and recreational plans. Tony's "service station" is his back-yard to which customers flock from far and wide.

<u>Manufacturer's Rep</u> – When office equipment salesman Charley Dresner decided to "cut down" at age 58, he assessed the seven man-ufacturers he had been representing for years. With his wife Gerda's help, he spent a weekend weeding out his three least profitable sup-pliers. Today, working twenty-five instead of forty-plus hours per week, he earns about 75 percent of his former income and the Dresners have time for other interests they never seemed able to get to in the past.

Construct Your "Guided Autobiography"

Dr. James E. Birren founded the gerontology program at the University of Southern California in 1965. At age 82 he is now associate director of the Center for Aging at U.C.L.A. "I haven't learned how to spell retirement yet," he says. With a sensible life's balance in mind, he has organized classes in "guided autobiography" which pinpoints the following 10 key areas of time commitment.

1. Family
2. Friends
3. Health and body
4. Homemaking
5. Career and work
6. Money
7. Education
8. Religion
9. Leisure and public service
10. Personal pursuits such as travel and crafts

How many of the Big Ten might you sell short if you go into business for yourself? Or if you mindlessly launch a new enterprise without a sensible life balance plan? It's a key point to consider.

Running your own show as an antidote to boredom

It is a healthy sociological sign that the population of ex-retirees appears to be mushrooming. For decades millions of people worked all their lives with a goal of retirement in mind. For a significant number, when that goal was achieved, retirement fell far short of what was anticipated. Inactivity, they discovered soon enough, can add up to boredom, depression, and declining health. Thus for many a new challenge presented itself: *How to get back into the mainstream and regain the rewards of intellectual and emotional stimulation that result in an active and productive life.*

Buying or starting a business, or resuming a former enterprise isn't the only cure for inactivity and boredom, but for some it's the ideal solution. Under the headline, BORED NO MORE, Florida *Sun-Sentinel* writer Marcia Heroux Pounds tells about Florida ex-retirees who quit the couch potato club for a crack at running their own businesses.

Tina and Graham Guthrie – The Guthries were sufficiently well heeled to afford a waterfront home in Highland Beach and a 32-foot Islander Catalina powerboat. But Tina especially, five years younger than her husband, soon became bored with "another sunny day in Florida." So they opened first one shop, Shell Game, then another, By the Sea Treasures, then a third, Galloping Seahorse, at various locations. They eventually consolidated and moved the enterprise to Delray Beach. "Like the pied piper," Pounds writes. Graham, who plays the piano, lures customers to the shop with refrains from Chopin and Scott Joplin. Tina finds the long hours exhaustive, but three days away on the boat she can't wait to get back.

Lee and Bernie Korol – Both college level educators, the Korols – Lee 67, Bernie 69 – soon wearied of their retirement lifestyle. All this education, Lee reasoned, and it's going to waste. On top of this, the Korols found their income wasn't sufficient to live as they wanted. Long interested in science (their daughter Donna is a neuroscientist), they purchased a franchise, Little Scientists, that offers a hands-on approach to teach science to children. The initial cost, $20,000, was higher than expected as it usually is, what with start-up costs for new programs, computer, supplies and whatnot. But they plan to pay off their original investment within a year. Once they train more teachers they can start building the business. Their only regret: Not having launched the enterprise 5 years earlier.

Fran Vogt-Strauss –Fran, 61, sold her marketing company in New Orleans and moved to Florida. After three months living on a yacht, Pounds reports, she became so bored she grumbled, "This is what you work for all your life." One day she saw neighbors cleaning their boat with a vacuum-like contraption called the Vapor Dragon. Intrigued by the machine, she bought a distributorship and applied her marketing skills to Fort Lauderdale-based Marketing 10 which distributes the commercial version and Vapor International which markets the household model. Despite four or five competitors on the scene, this savvy and gutsy entrepreneur claims about 50 percent of the market.

Three of Vogt-Strauss's sons, Scott, Matt, and Marc work in the business. "Having family in the firm has helped," she says, "because they are people you can trust." Sixty-hour per week work schedules may be more than she bargained for. But one thing is a certainty. She is no longer bored.

How old is too old to remain productively occupied? The archaic '65' guideline has long since lost its meaning. Relatively few seniors launch new enterprises at age 75, even fewer at 80. Does that mean 80 is too old? If you think so, expect an argument from Daisy Windsor of Oakland, Calif. who, at 97 still manages an apartment building, and recently passed her driving test to the applause of the licensing bureau personnel.

Selling your business? Rule out emotion realistically

The guy who comes to mind prefers to remain anonymous. For 30 years "Al" ran the profitable insurance agency he founded. At age 58 he decided to sell and stay on as a vice president in an advisory capacity and with a small financial interest in the business. The arrangement seemed to work for a month or so before it broke down. Al didn't know how to step down and when to butt out. He was outspokenly critical of every dumb decision that wasn't his. Of course, in his view, if it wasn't his it had to be a dumb decision. Frictions developed and multiplied. Shortly after, an agreement was reached that eased Al out of the agency.

Selling out isn't easy. Take it from someone who went through it more than once. When you're the big fish in the pond it's no fun to shrink down to a minnow. Years ago, as president of Steelcraft Manufacturing Company, a medium size enterprise, I was Honcho Numero Uno, the genius all the lesser lights reported to and were accountable to. I listened to the advice of my aides, but mine was the final word. The buck stopped at my throne. Ah, the pains of deflation.

When I sold Steelcraft to American Standard Inc. I abdicated my realm. My title diminished from chief executive to group vice president and the world suddenly changed. Much for the better as it turned out, but I had a tough emotional adjustment to make. I'm not ashamed of how I made it, but the transition from top dog to puppy could constitute a primer for what to expect when a business is sold. More years ago than I care to recall I wrote an article for *The President's Forum* titled "How To Become a Hired Hand and Like It." The points made in this piece apply no less strongly today. What follows is a sampling of lessons learned from hard experience on selling an enterprise and staying on to remain part of it.

Have you the humility to meek out?

Granted, you've been a super-savvy manager and decision-maker for years. But can you abide decisions made by others in the face of your better judgment? Can you face up to the realization first, that maybe, just maybe, you are not always right, and second, even if you *are* right you may have no choice but to swallow your righteousness? If you can't do that you might be better advised to step down altogether and check out other life options.

Can you get used to taking orders gracefully?

Face it, you're not the boss any more; you are now a subordinate, and subordinates are the guys who get bossed around. If you can't stomach that, a graceful exit might make more sense than hanging around.

Are you compatible with the top brass who will be running the show?

You don't have to *like* your new bosses. But if their personalities, politics, goals, and management style clash with your own, at one point or other an impasse will develop. While on the one hand, the elements of the arranged deal are important, selling your feelings and instincts short could result in problems down the road.

Has the buyer confided his or her plan for the company?

What new personnel will be brought in? How will this affect the lives and careers of key people who have been loyal and close to you for years? Does the buyer plan to expand, restructure, relocate, introduce new products, discontinue others? Will you be able to live comfortably with the changes contemplated?

What about other firms absorbed by the acquiring company?

How well have they fared? If problems are uncovered, have you any reason to expect you will fare differently?

The larger the acquired firm, the more complex the ramifications involved, the more important to address these and a host of other questions thoughtfully, and with the advice of an expert or two if need be.

Rekindlement Tip: "Many people dream of starting their own business after they retire. The smart way is to test the waters well in advance of retirement."

Think twice before taking a partner

As any management pro would agree, an enterprise is no better than the people who run it. Stories about would-be entrepreneurs who opened or purchased a bar only to have been "robbed blind" by the bartender are legend. Management consultant and educator Leonard J. Smith once told me, "The most risky business I know is the absentee ownership." George Ridley, an ace auto mechanic, at age 53 bought out his aging employer, and within two years more than doubled the profits of the three-bay service station.

One day he decided he was working too hard and set up first one, than another operation in other parts of town. The logistics and basic planning were right. The people operating it weren't. The two sub-stations *should have* been profitable. But unable to monitor the cash flow in and out closely enough, Ridley lost control of the operations and in time had to sell out. Moral of the story: If you're not sure of your partner and/or key people, you can't be sure of your bottom line.

Should You Pass the Business on to Your Kids?

It depends. Most of what it depends on is obvious. Although family businesses constitute more than half the nation's businesses, only 30 percent of them make it into the second generation as family enterprises, according to the Institute for Family Business at Nova Southeastern University. Critical questions arise: Should family members be accountable for the same performance and standards as non-family members? Should the same criteria for compensation exist for family and non-family members? Have your kids or other relatives had prior experience and involvement in the enterprise? Did they genuinely enjoy their involvement? Are they currently employees or shareholders? Do they share your wholehearted desire to perpetuate the enterprise? How would they feel if you sold the business rather than turned it over to them? What does your spouse think about it? Do her feelings and yours coincide?

Ralph Funeral Home – Fifty-something Tom Ralph gets calls weekly about selling his business, a Florida *Sun-Sentinel* feature story reports. Ralph doesn't even consider the proposed offers although he himself expects to step down within the next few years. The reason can be spelled out in one word: **ENTHUSIASM**, the ultimate key to success in any enterprise you could name. Four of Ralph's kids are enthusiastically involved in the business. Even his 6-year-old grandson gets excited. He recently exulted, "Grandpa, I'm going to own this business some day." For the Ralphs the prognosis looks good.

Heartland Lumber Co. – "I wouldn't mind bringing my son and daughter into the business," 54 year-old Ben Larkin says. "But if I have to twist their arms to do so, fugheddaboutit." Ben Junior is into ecology and is a sociology major. He expresses his regrets candidly, "Sorry, Dad, but business just isn't my thing." Dorothy, who is working on her second novel, is no less frank. "They're adults," Larkin says sensibly. "You gotta respect their wishes and ambitions." In a year or two he plans to sell the firm and go into what he refers to as semi-retirement, with heady renewal goals on the agenda.

Atlantic Floorcovering Inc. – Joe Morse's two sons and a daughter, 28, 30, and 33 respectively, already involved in the retail business, all but threaten manslaughter if their father sells out. But Joe and his wife Anne have already decided that sell they will. "There would be no point in discussing this with the kids," they agree, "what would ensue is a riot." The reason is clear. The kids have strong personalities of their own and are super-ambitious. They don't get along, are at each other's throats constantly. The only thing they agree on is that the other two aren't qualified in general and for the top slot in particular. Morse confides that the "family business" is a shade short of bedlam. It's one of the reasons he wants out.

So "All In the Family", while a super TV series, may or may not work out if what you have in mind is a family enterprise. Given the right circumstances, a family business with its inherent components of trust, loving and care could be an ideal setting for a life of productive and enjoyable rekindlement with gradual phase-out as it meets your time commitment expectations and needs. Given the wrong circumstances, it could be a disaster.

For some better alternative

Entrepreneurship isn't for everyone. Or maybe it is if you take consultant Leonard J. Smith's counsel to heart. Smith believes, "Entrepreneur or not, you should work as if you're self-employed." An interesting concept which, in the consultant's opinion, can't miss. "After all," he [points out, "employer or employee, absolute security in corporate America doesn't exist."

Despite the much publicized rush to self-employment in the 90's, today there is a less touted flock from entrepreneurship back to the payroll. Smith cites the following reasons (among others) for tossing in the entrepreneurial sponge.

"I didn't realize how hard I would have to work."

"I found out early on that I was the only really caring guy on the team."

"I kept pouring more and more money into the enterprise. It

was beginning to reach a point of no return."

"I find that I sleep much better at night on a payroll than when meeting the payroll was my responsibility."

"I thought I'd be able to get out and sell my company and its ideas. Instead, I found myself bogged down in the office."

"I just don't have the balls. Despite all the frustrations involved, I never worried so much as an employee as I did when I ran my own firm."

"My most humbling admission, I guess, is that I'm just not smart enough to run my own enterprise."

Is running your own show for you? Given the pros and cons, that's for you to decide. If you're constituted to do so, go for it.

108

Chapter 7

Practice Dollar Diplomacy

Making Financial and Life Plans Compatible

"If you took all the experience and judgment of men over fifty out of the world, there wouldn't be enough left to run it."

Henry Ford

I'm not going to use that nasty word, retirement. But, hopefully, you've been sufficiently brainwashed by now to: 1. Plan hard and thoughtfully for your rekindlement years. Or, more specifically, with this chapter in mind, for the day when that regular paycheck will stop coming in, and 2. Get started well in advance in deciding how you want to spend the rest of your life and how best to fulfill your wishes and needs. No one said it was easy, but everyone seems to agree it is necessary.

The Big Question

You see it all over the place. Read a newspaper or magazine article. Listen to a TV or radio pitch. Pick up a book with the ugly R word in its title, and you can't miss it: HOW MUCH MONEY MUST YOU SAVE FOR RETIREMENT? It's a good question. Whether your intention is to save for rekindlement or its inactive alternative, boredom, you will still need X number of dollars to live on, have fun with, and accomplish your goals, when the paymaster crosses your name from his list. So what's the next step? You turn to the experts, what else? . With the help of charts, actuarial tables, surveys, and calculators, these guys will provide the life blueprint you need. Right? Well, let's see.

Experts' Response – Opinion Type One

- Annual "Retirement Conference" Survey: "...few (people) still have any idea how much money they will need or have even tried to figure it out..."

- Employee Benefit Research Institute: "...only slightly more than one in four workers, or 27 percent, have any idea how much they will need to retire when they want, the way they want..." "Less than one-third of Americans 53 and older and only 27 percent of those between 45 and 52 have saved more than $100,000 for retirement, according to the survey..." "...a retiree who puts $100,000 into a lifetime annuity today is likely to receive about $886 a month in income, or $10,632 a year, just at the poverty level for a family of two..."

- *Newsweek* Article: "Merrill Lynch weighs in annually with its version of bleakness. The latest: boomers are saving only 38 cents for every retirement dollar they'll need. Researchers at the Wharton School have told pre-retirees they must save 16 percent of their incomes between now and the age of 62 to make it through their golden years..."

- Study for Mutual-fund Companies Fidelity and Scudder: "...six out of 10 boomers...have no idea how much savings they will need (when they reach 65)..."

- Banker: "Most people I know in their fifties underestimate by 60 percent or more how much they will need when that regular paycheck stops coming in.

- Calculator: "Compare this device with your current savings objective and you will probably find you are putting your future at risk..."

Experts' Response – Opinion Type Two

- Financial Expert Jane Bryant Quinn: "How much should you save to retire at your current standard of living? To answer that question, many of us turn to a retirement worksheet or calculator. But they tend to overestimate what you're really going to need. You'll save more than you have to, if you follow what they say..."

- Accountant: "Considering inherited money, accumulated interest, and continuing earnings, in my experience many people in their fifties are over-anxious and paranoid about planning their future..."

- Estate Planner: "Too many wealthy people from what I have seen are restrictively limited in targeting how much they will need; if they follow their plan to the letter they will become scrunchy old penny-pinchers..."

- Financial Executive: "Thousands of people seem to be functioning under the premise that Social Security and Medicare will fold up and go home one of these days. I don't believe it; if they fold something else will take their place. This isn't India."

- Consultant: "In my experience, except on rare occasions, nest eggs don't crash; they harden up and grow bigger."

- Banker: "Plan, by all means, but don't go overboard. Don't live too frugally for the sake of your kids. It's true, older people need less to live on: No more mortgage payments, less clothing, travel, change cars less frequently, less keeping up with the Joneses; in general, they make do for less. But that doesn't mean they should scrimp and scrape for their kids."

So there you have it. A choice awaits you. One from column A, one from column B. Are you an optimist, pessimist, or simply down-to-earth sensible?

The disparity of expert opinion should be no surprise to anyone. Many, if not most, of the key planning factors are fraught with uncertainty. How can you properly anticipate or project *anything* if you can't rely on the basic figures involved in your plan?. Consider the following list of factors that will over the long pull determine your lifestyle and what will be affordable five, 10, 20 and more years down the pike. Then ask yourself: How many of these figure can you know in advance? How many will remain unchanged and stable?

- Your stock market investments.
- Your wages and salary.
- The after-payroll-checks tax bite.
- Marketplace demand for older workers.
- Possibility of being downsized.
- Amount of inherited money.
- Possible ravages of inflation on savings.
- Fluctuating rate of return for investments and savings.
- Home equity.
- Your Social Security payments. (How much and at what age available)
- Your Medicare needs.
- Your Medicare payments.
- Your family's state of health.
- The mushrooming cost of drugs.
- Your children's financial needs.
- Your grandkids' financial needs.
- Possible relocation.
- Changing personal desires and goals.
- Payback to society – volunteerism.
- Your longevity.

How many of the above factors can you predict accurately decades into the future?

Solidly sold as I am on thoughtful and thorough advance planning for how much money one will need to live on when the regular paychecks stop flowing, it is still important to keep in mind what motivates experts whose advice on the subject is for sale. On the one hand, I can't fault the better-safe-than-sorry approach. On the other, it's obvious that if you can be frightened into worrying that you are likely to be caught short if you don't take some fast planning action, you will be more receptive to the pitch of a financial consultant.

The Rel Step Planning System

I said it wasn't easy, and judging from the disparity in their projections, the only thing the experts reach consensus on with regard to planning for when the paycheck stops coming is that indeed, planning is necessary. I couldn't agree more. It's more than necessary. It's absolutely essential. What's more, planning should start, not when you're about to fall into the soup, but *before you even pick up the spoon!* Do you want me to be specific? Alright, here it is.

The question is, with dollar diplomacy in mind, if the experts can't agree on how you will spend your rekindlement life generally and your financial life particularly in years to come, how are you supposed to figure it out how to do it for yourself? Actually, it's not too hard if you have the right mindset. See if the REL Step Planning System (REL-SPS). makes sense to you. It's as easy as tying your shoe. Here's how it works.

IF YOU ARE PAST FIFTY AND YOU HAVE NOT BEGUN AS YET TO PLAN HOW YOU WANT TO SPEND THE NEXT 25 TO 30 YEARS OF YOUR LIFE, YOU ARE OFF TO A LATE START!

Robert E. Levinson

First: You Have To Face the Realities

Bob and Ethel Baumgarten – A decade ago, in their mid-fifties, the only plans the Baumgartens had ever made for the future was Bob's more or less tentative decision to step down from his auditing job at age 62. The thought of how much money they would need to live on after that never entered their heads.

Like most people, if there was one thing they steered clear of thinking about it was how much money they would inherit when Ethel's mom and dad died. And they would certainly never bring up the subject. While their parents were still alive, their assets and bank accounts were strictly Mom's and Dad's own business. "But let's face it," Ethel reasoned one day, "My parents are loaded. Even if the inheritance is split evenly between my brother and me, we'll eventually come into a bundle."

Bob agreed. Dad's manufacturing business had flourished for years. Ethel's parents owned an expensive home, high priced cars and jewelry, had traveled lavishly since Dad's business was sold. Money was of small concern to them. "We'll get a million at least," Bob figured. "More than that," Ethel said.

Bob resigned his job at 62, and devoted most of his time to golf, tennis, cultural pursuits, and volunteer work. Ethel took up golf, and also did volunteer work. Their combined savings and investments at the time were a shade under $100,000, enough they calculated, "to live comfortably on."

Unfortunately, it didn't work out that way. Ethel's mom died first after a long, costly, and underinsured illness. Within six months her dad remarried and died six months later. The Baumgartens' total share of the split inheritance was $6,500. Their rapidly eroding assets were not enough to live on. They sold their house and moved into a small apartment. Bob was lucky to get part time work. Ethel can no longer afford a weekly cleaning woman. At the supermarket she scrounges.

The point makes itself. Whatever appearances might be, no one can project or predict with accuracy what the future will be. Inheritance expectation is only one of several factors.

The Worst Planning Scenario

Along with mistaken projections of inheritance windfalls, two of the biggest financial planning doozies people make, according to a *Wall Street Journal* report, are underestimating the role of inflation and longevity. Will today's low inflation rate persist fifteen or 20 years from today? Assuming you are healthy, your guess is no better than your doctor's with regard to how long you will live. If the inflation rate reverts to double or triple today's it could chop your income expectation in half or worse.

As any savvy computer pro could confirm: No system or procedure can be any more effective or useful than the input that goes into it. *Garbage In, Garbage Out* (Gi-Go) as an old IBMer friend of mine used to put it. That's why REL-SPS is so simple. A quick look at what goes into the typical plan concocted by a typical adviser, network financial engine, calculator, chart, table, or whatever will soon spell out in clear terms why mindless conventional planning won't work. *Unless!!!* -- and that's the crux of this relatively effortless system – *Unless!!!* The plan is duplicated repeatedly.
Ethel's projection of an inheritance of one million-plus is a fine example of Garbage In. With Gi-Go in mind, the key point to latch on to is that:

It is senseless to assume that the figures and projections – the input – you feed into your plan today, will apply to your life and lifestyle fifteen or 20 years down the pike. Some are unlikely to hold firm even five or 10 years from the time you set your plan on paper. So how could you expect them to have dependable meaning today? *Unless you opt for Variable Planning. A Step at a Time – to be updated using current projections every two or years or so.* In other words, when the sands keep shifting, it makes no sense to try to set your two feet in concrete? Applying REL-SPS to your future, there is no need to do so. As times change, along with the state of the economy and your personal fortunes, inclinations, and goals, your plan should be updated accordingly. I don't suggest that you ignore or pooh pooh the experts; *you should simply tailor their know-how and advice to the significant changes in your life on an ongoing basis.*

What Help Can You Get From the Experts?

Are your assets and nest egg substantial and complex? If so, it might make sense to invest in the probably expensive planning advice of an established financial consultant. I neither suggest nor reject this option. Just keep in mind that not even the most sophisticated experts know with any degree of accuracy how the items on the above checklist will change over the years. If you decide to do your own planning, retail and library bookshelves are lined with books on the subject. The American Association for Retired People (AARP) makes available all kinds of helpful planning tips and assistance. Almost daily, articles on the financial aspects of survival in one's later years are published in *The Wall Street Journal, The New York Times,* and your local newspapers. A sampling of typical titles follows:

- HOW GOOD IS YOUR PLAN?
- STUDY: BOOMERS NOT PLANNING FOR RETIREMENT
- GOLDEN YEARS? MAYBE NOT
- MONEY ISN'T EVERYTHING
- RETIRE EARLY? DREAM ON
- THERE ARE NO EASY ANSWERS TO PLANNING FOR RETIREMENT
- THE GOLDEN FEARS
- TIME TO QUIT – BUT HOW?
- DECISIONS, DECISIONS
- BOOMERS MAY HAVE NO DESIRE TO RETIRE
- RETIRED WORKERS A VALUABLE ASSET
- CALCULATORS MAY BE OVERSHOOTING THE MARK
- EARLY RETIREMENT?
- TOO MUCH, TOO LITTLE... JUST RIGHT
- DON'T FORGET THE TAX BITE AT RETIREMENT
- PROTECTING THE NEST EGG

And so on and on.

Where the Money Comes From

What are the major sources of income for people age 65 and over? Here, according to the Administration on Aging and Census Bureau, are the rankings one to 5.

1. Social Security
2. Pensions
3. Asset Income
4. Earnings
5. Other

Finally, you can get a virtual education on how to invest and remain solvent when your paychecks stop coming from the Internet. And much, if not most of it – if you ignore the commercial ax being ground – is for free. For example:

WWW.VANGUARD.COM – Under the heading, **Retirement Planning Basics,** Vanguard offers a planning course that almost literally runs from A to Z. The course, not surprisingly, focuses largely on various groups and types of investments. It lists several articles, defines different kinds of investments and spells out risks involved. It includes Types of Retirement Savings Plans, lists books and websites for investors, and cites recommended resources.

WWW.FIDELITY.COM -- Fidelity's retirement section on its home page is headed, **Retirement...Life after work ...are you ready?** Despite my basic premise that in too many cases "life after work" means vegetation, Fidelity's website is well worth visiting and will give you something to think about. One especially useful section is titled "Good Habits of Effective Retirement Savers". Also, investment advice for Retirement Plan Participants, Individual Investors, Financial Advisors, Plan Sponsors, and Small Business Owners.

WWW.SCHWAB.COM – Schwab's website is headed **Retirement Saving Made Simple.** It offers a Retirement Savings Planner along with all kinds of good advice about investing in IRAs and elsewhere. The website concludes with a quote from Charles R.

Schwab himself: "As a rule of thumb, for every five years you wait, you may need to double your monthly investing amount to reach the same goal."

WWW.FINANCIALENGINES.COM – *Newsweek* columnist Jane Bryant Quinn, one of the best of the lot, writes of FE: "It is the brainchild of Nobel economist William Sharpe and – uniquely among Web calculators – gives you a feel for your investments' chance of success." There are no guarantees, she says, but this is a service worth testing. FE's Website opens with the question, "Will I have enough money when I retire?" It continues, "We FORECAST what your investments might be worth in the future. We provide unbiased ADVICE to help you make better investment decisions. We MONITOR your investments to help you stay on track.

One more time: Planning for how much money you will need to live on when the flow of wage income stops isn't easy. But the biggest mistake you could make is *not* to plan, and the second biggest mistake you could make is to start planning too late. The third biggest mistake? Formulating a plan, and then neglecting to review and reevaluate it regularly.

Why do so many people, boomers and others, fail to plan for their future at all? Among the most common reasons given are:

- It's too complicated.
- I don't have the time.
- My budget is too tight to put any money away.
- Retirement is too far off to worry about it.

Although these and other websites are well worth exploring, keep one key thought in mind: Whether you opt for retirement or renewal there's a lot more to financial planning for the future than how you will invest your money. The idea is to include in your plan everything that is important to you, and to bear in mind that, like everything else in life, your values are subject to change as well. Holding on to this thought, I recommend that you...

...Do it! Then do it again and again

Pick the plan of your choice – from a book, chart, magazine article, financial consultant, *Wall Street Journal* advisory, or brokerage firm – T. Rowe Price (WWW.Troweprice.com) has a particularly good one – then mark a date on your bulletin board to review and update it every two years. By the time your paychecks run out you will be ready and raring to go.

Responsibility for your kids: How much? How long?

"If I Only Had It To Do Over!"

Tom Grant (name disguised), the friend who confided this lament, was almost tearful at the time. His story is not all that uncommon. Executive vice president of a major manufacturing company, at age 56 he was on a career roll and well heeled. Tom was a manufacturing guru. As such the reality that he had manufactured a bum was a painful pill to swallow. Tom Jr., age 37, had everything a kid could desire: pricey car, expensive clothes, spending money galore. Except that he was no longer a kid. What Tom lacked was an occupation, or an interest in anything other than clubbing, partying, and one-night stands. 'Spoiled rotten' might be another way to put it. His only redeeming feature, his father told me, was that he wasn't on drugs. Or at least not yet.

Tom Jr.'s problem was that he couldn't see the point of working for what he perceived to be the goodies of life if he could get them for free. He had gone through an embarrassing 5-month stint in the sales department of Dad's company. His father had arranged a sequence of jobs through friends, myself included; all had turned out to be disasters. 'If I only had it to do over!' his dad said. That was about two years ago. It was too late to do over. The "kid" had already been shaped and formed. The last I heard from Tom Sr. he had lost touch with his son.

I've seen it happen time and again. We are, of course, responsible for our children. But where does responsibility end? I believe we are responsible for caring for them, for showing them love, for encouraging their love and caring for others, for acting as role models to the best of our ability, for sheltering them and providing opportunities for their education and growth. But beyond that? There must come a time when young people have to strike out on their own having, hopefully, been given the equipment to do so. Showering them with wannagets, from what I have seen, is usually more hurtful than helpful. Tom Sr. worked for his bounty and earned every cent of it. In my experience, there is no viable alternative I know to working and earning to achieve one's goals. Some day, with God's blessing, Tom Jr. may learn this the hard way.

I have seen too many people like my friend Tom, in their fifties, 60s and 70s, sacrificing their own needs and desires to make life easy for their grown-up kids. In my view, however well-meaning they may be, they overlook the vital parental responsibility of helping, guiding, and teaching their kids to strike out on their own with dignity and self-respect – to work for and earn what they get.

The Couple Who Responded To a Wake-Up Call

Nothing can be more gratifying than to see your good counsel take hold and enhance somebody's lifestyle. Ed Brown (name disguised) age 61, worked for me about ten years ago. Unlike Tom Grant, he wasn't a wealthy man; he was what could be called "comfortably fixed." But pinchpenny! He made Scrooge look like a spendthrift.

A talented engineer, Ed's lifelong hobby and pride was woodworking or, more specifically, cabinet making. Ed actually designed and built the furniture – chairs, rockers, cocktail tables, book cases, etc. His wife Irma, equally talented, did the finishing. The Brown's basement was loaded with exquisite pieces. One day Ed came to me for advice. He and his wife Irma were torn. They had been nursing a dream for years, to start their own little woodworking business, and vacation and travel when they felt like it. They'd already had some success selling units to neighbors and a retailer in the area.

"So what's the problem?" I asked.

The problem turned out to be their children. Joe, on a social worker's job, was struggling; Edna wasn't much better off. Her husband was periodically in and out of work. "They're going to need every penny they can get when we die."

No argument for self-sacrifice distresses me more. I tried to impress on him the right he and Irma had to pursue their own goal, the *responsibility* they had to themselves to live out their lives fruitfully and productively. Ed agreed that made sense. But he looked skeptical.

"Do me a favor," I said. "Talk to Harry down at the bank. Tell him what you told me and see what he says."

He agreed to do so. The following year Ed resigned. The Browns' little business began to thrive from the outset and is still going strong. They take periodic vacations and major trips when they want to. Their kids are still struggling, and Ed and Irma lend a financial hand from time to time. It's the best they can do and as well as anyone could be expected to do.

As Florida-based financial columnist Humberto Cruz states the case: "How much money you need in retirement (or rekindlement) also will vary greatly depending on whether you opt to 'die broke,' that is, deplete your savings during your lifetime, or prefer to leave your savings principal untouched as a safety net or to leave to your heirs, or make a choice in between these two extremes." My personal choice: I am not an extremist.

Abrupt Departures Can Be Costly

The handwriting is on the wall and you're a speed reader. If you're about to be retired or downsized, the following delaying tactics might just possibly work:

Propose a drastic salary reduction with a corresponding cut in working hours.

Company's Advantage: Payroll burden is reduced; yet your talent and know-how are still available.

Your Advantage: You still enjoy use of office space, secretary, telephone, etc., without the out-of-pocket cost you'll incur once you're gone.

Ask your boss to keep you on the books in a consulting or ad hoc capacity.

Company's Advantage: You will be on hand when you're needed; the company meets its cost-cutting objective while retaining your special know-how and skill.

Your Advantage: You're still an insider. It's easier to reconnect while accessible at place of employment.

Make known your availability as vacation time or peak period fill-in, etc.

Company's Advantage: Again, cost-cutting objective is achieved, without the loss of your valuable training, know-how, and experience.

Your Advantage: Your time will be largely your own, but with facilities intact to pursue other contacts, opportunities, and options at will.

This doesn't mean you can swing a special deal for yourself with your boss. *But it doesn't hurt to ask.* Most people when retired or downsized kiss off without another thought and almost immediately are stunned by after-tax expenses for facilities and benefits they always took for granted. I could cite numerous cases of men and women downsized or retired who, after a chat with their boss, were kept on under one special deal or another. "Nothing ventured…" You fill in the rest.

Should you quit? If so, when?

Fortunately, or perhaps unfortunately, depending on your perspective, people in their fifties and 60s are in an excellent position to resign their jobs if they wish, or hang in there another five, 10, or more years. As *Newsweek* columnist Robert J. Samuelson states the case: "Companies – facing a scarcity of younger workers – may need more older workers." So, if you want to hang on past sixty-five or 70, the odds are good you will be welcome.

But that can be a tough decision to make. A former business associate, age 59, was wondering whether to throw in the sponge. "For the first time in my life," he told me, "I'm in a position to spend a lot of time with my wife."

My response was quick and to the point. "Unless your situation is unusual, I can think of no worse reason to opt for early retirement."

"Look," I added, "I couldn't begin to imagine the disruption my sudden and unexpected availability would inflict on Phyllis's day-to-day schedule of projects, programs, volunteer work and recreational activity. She loves me dearly, but her inevitable reaction would most certainly be, 'That would be all I need!'"

Moral of the story: Think twice, then once again, before turning your comfortable and established lifestyle upside down.

Deborah – "Honey, it's now or never. If you want me to teach you the business, come into the firm. Or else, I'll sell it."
Deborah, 50, had long resisted Dad's urging. A succession of secretarial and supervisory jobs had proved her merit, but if she came in with Dad now she could double her income. She liked advertising, but was it worth the price? Dad was a tough boss, set in his ways. Fiercely independent, Deborah had long been determined to do things her way. With Dad this wouldn't be easy. But as he said, it was now or never. What to do?
Dad was in no less of a what-to-do quandary. If Deborah decided to join the firm, at age 74 he would throw in the towel in a year or two, turn over the reins, and follow long postponed pursuits. But what if she decided against it? Would he continue to hang in there? If so, for how long?

"It Ain't Over Till It's Over"

Innumerable questions like these plague millions of people. You worked hard all your life and have plenty to show for it. Enough is enough, right? This rationale made sense to friends and relatives of Post Master General Marvin Runyon, 73, who urged him to retire after six years of distinguished service with the Post Office, years as CEO of Nissan Motors USA, chairman of the Tennessee Valley Authority, and before that 37 years as a Ford Motor Co. vice president. "How many careers do you want?" he was asked. "Two more," Runyon replied, who believes with Yogi Berra that it ain't over till it's over."

Virginia Snyder agrees. Being tagged as a little old lady may not seem like enviable status to some. But to the "Gumshoe Granny" – interviewed on Dave Letterman's *Late Night* and NBC's *Today Show* -- it has clear advantages. Head of her own private detective agency at age 77, Snyder isn't about to give up. Why should she? She loves every minute of it. When it comes to nailing miscreants, no disguise could be more effective. "South Florida is full of us!" she chortles. "Working with her husband, Ross, 77, and nephew K. Wayne Campbell," *People* Magazine reports, "Snyder charges $50 an hour plus expenses to investigate everything from the backgrounds of potential employees to the gory details of murders." She helped overturn the 1984 murder conviction of Willie Brown by tracking down an ex-con who admitted to having given false testimony. She has run-ins with cops when she digs into a case and critiques their investigative techniques. She doesn't hesitate to sue the establishment when she feels she is right.

Last I heard Snyder is as active as ever and writing two books in her spare time. No way am I about to settle into a rocking chair, she proclaims. "I'm my own boss, and I love it. I'll never be torn with guilt because I didn't do enough."

What if you have had enough?

It might be at age fifty, 60, 70 or later. But at same point in your life, realities being what they are, the time will come when you will have to ask yourself if enough is enough. Faced with this decision, critical considerations erupt. Are you posing the question because:

- You're fed up with your job or your business and can't stand it any more?

- You have physical problems and feel, or have been told by your doctor that continuing to work will be detrimental to your health?
- You have other pursuits you've been yearning to follow and decide if you don't do it now you will never do it?
- Family pressures to throw in the career sponge have been getting to you?
- Someone has approached you with an attractive work alternative you feel you can't afford to turn down?

Jim Dowling – For over thirty years Jim has supervised an assembly line in a cosmetics plant. Ask him how he feels about his job, and the venom oozes out of him. He finds it hard to describe what he hates more: Supervising twelve men and women with low to mediocre morale, or the day-to-day, week-to-week boredom. At age 62 he decides that he's had it. The problem is that Beth and Jim's financial planning has left something to be desired; if Jim quits now, before too many years they may find themselves financially strapped. Beth is sympathetic to Jim's feelings and plight, but she has a suggestion. "Why not talk to Mr. Simpson? Maybe he'll agree to let you cut down your hours." Jim doubted it but agreed he had nothing to lose. After thinking it over, Mr. Simpson decided he didn't want to lose a man as skilled and hardworking as Jim who now works 25 hours a week. Surprise! Suddenly he doesn't hate his job any more.

Chester Leibman – Chester, age 50, is a loader on the company's No. 3 dock. His doctor couldn't have been more blunt. "Chet, with your heart condition, I couldn't predict another five years if that heavy lifting continues." "I can't afford to quit," he replied. His doctor shrugged. "It's your choice. You've been twenty years with that outfit, right? I'm sure if you explained the situation they would find a lighter job for you." "Sure, at a third less pay." "A third less pay is better than a third less life." Like it or not, Leibman had no choice but to accept his doctor's advice.

Alice Markham – When George Markham died, Alice, 52, made four crucial decisions: 1. She hated cold weather and decided to move to San Diego. 2. She had accumulated a nice nest egg from the profitable men's fashion store she and George had run for 22 years, but derived no real satisfaction from it and decided to sell. 3. She was tired of her adult children overburdening her with their problems and decided she had lived too close to them for too long. 4. Healthy and sensuous, she concluded that widowhood wasn't for her. Today, a year after George's demise, she already has acted upon decisions one, two, and three, and is hard at work on number four.

Jason Murdoch – "Jay, we don't need the money. Isn't it time you sold the agency so that we can begin to enjoy the fruits of your work?" Murdoch, 59, had been hearing this refrain from Marge and the kids for the past four or five years. Trouble was he loved the challenges of his successful small insurance agency, didn't mind the long hours, had visited enough museums and monastaries all over the world to last him a lifetime, and wasn't a fun and games kind of person. He responded well to the challenges of business and had a ball doing it. Six months ago Marge left him. They are still good friends, and they both enjoy life more.

Grace Withers – Grace, 49, advanced on her job with a medium size accounting firm from executive secretary to training director at a salary of $85,000 a year. Arlene, a close friend, heads a small but profitable secretarial school in New York City. "Grace, if you can do it for someone else, you can do it for yourself." It was the second time Arlene offered her a partnership in her business. This time she took her up on it. "Best decision I ever made," she confides.

Perhaps the most critical question facing you when you feel ready to quit is: Cold turkey, or the go-slow approach? Of course, not everyone has this alternative. But from what I have seen, waking up with no workplace to go to and no paycheck to look forward to, can be a numbing experience. In most cases, cold turkey is as much to be avoided if possible when walking out on a job as it is on Thanksgiving. The slow, part time approach to rekindlement has much to be said for it.

Chapter 8
Take Time for Yourself

Starting now

"Everyone thinks of changing society and nobody thinks of changing himself."

Leo Tolstoy

For 89 years Brewster, Mass. Resident Eugenie "Genie" Garside suffered from a self-imposed stigma that said she would never get a high school degree. At 98, she had other problems as well such as her hip, knee, and hearing. But in recent years at least, despite the hardship, whether triggered by a rude awakening or whatever, Genie turned into a fighter. At age 98, reports *Cape Cod Times* staff writers Robin Lord and Paul Gauvin, with the help of a walker, she "was awarded a diploma from (Nauset Regional High School) to sustained applause, hoots and hollers from a wall-to-wall audience."

Garside left school at age 9 in 1909 because she was needed at home to help care for her ailing stepmother and 11 younger siblings. But her will to learn never abated. Despite her lack of schooling she resolutely tackled and mastered the French language when she moved to Montreal. Receiving a high school diploma was no more than an unattainable goal until she confessed her dream to Catherine Tarr, a Pleasant Bay Nursing and Rehabilitation staff member nearby. Tarr recruited willing students to tutor the plucky lady in English, math, science, history, geography and spelling. "I'm still a lousy speller," she admits, but she passed.

"How do you feel about college?" she was asked.

"If I get this much attention, why not?"

View TODAY As The Starting Point In Your Life

If you are 50, 60, or 70 and believe you are "too old" to drastically and significantly change your life, call Genie Garside to mind and think again. Think again and sign up as a charter member of the Robert E. Levinson Society To Expose 65 As a Fraud. When I began writing this book, I conceptualized age 65 as life's starting point instead of a preface to its closure. I have since altered my judgment. I now feel that if 65 is a starting point, no better plan or strategy could be devised than to get a *head start* at age 55. No better time can I think of – after working your butt off for others all these years – to start thinking in terms of doing what you want for yourself.

What If What You Want Is What You Already Have?

Working your butt off can be positive or negative enterprise depending on your state of mind. At age 60 or 70, for example, you may decide you've had it, or you may want more of the same. At 65 Richard Levy, a highly productive partner in the big prestigious Chicago law firm, Kirkland & Ellis, wanted more of the same, according to *Wall Street Journal* reporter Paul M. Barrett. But K&E didn't want more of him unless he agreed to relinquish his lucrative partnership and become a salaried employee. Either that or bon jour. Mr. Levy wasn't happy with his choices. Billing banking and real estate clients, he had earned more than $900,000 the previous year, $1 million the year before that.

With this kind of smarts and experience he was anything but "washed up," and with a little hard research and effort, he reasoned, it shouldn't be hard to find an employer smart and imaginative enough to cash in on his income producing potential. The firm Levy switched to, Altheimer & Gray, may be a cut behind K&E, 210 lawyers instead of 500, but its policy is to snap up gray-haired veterans so long as they add to the pie instead of subtracting from it.

Levy's reputation for forging clever and wily deals was all it took

to sell A&G on his value. "Mr. Levy says he is already billing more than $3 million on a annualized basis," Barrett reports, and "his partnership share is expected to be more than $500,000."
He brought not only his expertise to his new employer but such clients as Bank of America Illinois, and National Bank of Yugoslavia, among others.

How do the law firm's younger partners feel about the infusion into its partnership ranks of veterans like Levy? Peter Lieberman, 34, tells about the time he got bogged down in talks over the breakup of a $60 million real estate partnership. Roused from sleep by a midnight phone call, Levy cheerfully gave him the guidance he needed to pull the fox out of the chicken coop. "He made me look strong," says Lieberman. "Of course I'm glad to have him around."

Valdas Adamkus

"Enough is enough," he decided a couple of years ago after decades of government service, his latest stint as a high level bureaucrat in the Environmental Protection Agency. Mr. Adamkus looked forward to "golden" years of retirement, perfecting his golf swing, puttering around in the garden.

His wife didn't believe it. No way could Val sit around doing next to nothing. Alma was smart enough to understand that years are not made golden by retirement but by a gutsy crack at renewal, and it didn't take her husband long to acknowledge it. Having fled Lithuania a half century before as a freedom fighter, he long had dreamed of some day returning. Well, what better time? Miracle of miracles! How does the axiom go – Where there's a will…?

Not only did Valdas Adamkus return, but he did so as president of Lithuania after a court ruled that his many visits over the years qualified him as a candidate. Moral of the story: No dream is impossible given the motivation to achieve it.

Ellen Lender

Big dreams, or little dreams, inspirational role models help.

When Harry's faltering heart finally gave in, his wife of 40 years became depressed and panicky with feelings of helplessness. Added to this was her recent layoff from her administrative job.

Her caring daughter Sue's help was a blessing. "Mom, you're a smart active woman, not a poolside potato. You spent your whole life doing for others, your kids, Dad, the community. It's time to start thinking about yourself. You've got decades of good life ahead of you if you put your mind to it. What you need is a change of mindset and attitude."

In an effort to cheer her up, Sue gave Mom a copy of comedian Alan King's fourth book, "Name Dropping," the life and lives of Alan King. Ellen long had enjoyed King. She couldn't put it into words, but something in his nature and outlook, a kind of never-say-die quality, appealed to her. After decades of playing for laughs, he wasn't afraid to try something different. He started appearing in films: As a rabbi in an HBO moves, "The Infiltrator," as a mobster in Martin Scorcese's film, "Casino." He stars in an HBO program, "Alan King: Inside the Comedy Mind." He founded the Alan King Diagnostic Medical Center in Jerusalem.

Sue's message got through: Put your mind to it and you can do anything you decide you can do. So Ellen began to set goals for herself: Overcome boredom, learn to use the computer, land a new job to preserve her financial independence – pair up with a likable guy to end the devastation of loneliness.

Impossible task? Not with Ellen's powerful attributes: Good physical health, natural enthusiasm, common sense fueled by years of business experience and, like Alan King, once she set her mind to it, an unflappable can-do attitude.

Ellen introduced herself to the Internet and fell in love with it. In a Seniors Chat Group she met – and now lives with – Man Number Two of her dreams.

Find a Need and Fill It

Better still, fill a need that ties in to your life's experience. Once in the Navy, the sea gets into your blood. So it was only natural that after a 20-year career, retired commander, Milt Baker and his wife set sail for points far and wide on the foamy blue. Then one day on their way to the Bahamas they pulled into Fort Lauderdale to pick up some nautical charts. None were available because they couldn't find a store that specialized in them.

That was the end of retirement. Just as well. Things were beginning to get humdrum. "The Bakers," reports John Chiu in the Fort Lauderdale *Sun-Sentinel*, "decided to invest their life's savings in this untapped market." That was 15 years ago. Today Bluewater Books & Charts stocks more than 25,000 paper nautical charts that cover the world, and provides electronic charts as well. The Bakers live on the *Selchie*, a Cabo Rico 38 footer and last year chalked up sales of $4 million. A computer network keeps them up to date on which charts are in demand. Bluewater's knowledgeable staff, most of whom spent years in the marine industry, Baker feels, is the secret of the firm's success.

Not so secret is the combination of expertise and a need that cries to be filled. Right on, Commander!

21ˢᵗ Century rekindlement Internet Style

I recently engaged in an intriguing conversation with Bill Ireland, 74, a friend in the real estate business. Having heard I was writing an antiretirement book, he thought I might be interested in some thoughts he'd been mulling.

"About what?" I inquired.

"Friendship. Socializing."

"What about friendship, socializing?"

He grinned. "Well, I can't help comparing two or three decades ago with today."

Bill's a smart guy, with an active mind. "I'm all ears."

"Okay, this is the gist of it. Thinking back a couple of decades, how many people would you say were in your circle of friends? Not counting business associates."

"Hey, come on, Bill. I don't have a count. Several, I suppose."

"Give me a guesstimate; I won't hold you to it. I'm trying to make a point."

I shrugged. "A few close friends, I guess. Maybe a couple of dozen or more not so close friends and casuals."

"Located where?

"Mostly nearby. Those who move away you lose track of. You write or call for a while, then gradually stop. You exchange cards on holidays, but the relationship deteriorates into little more than a memory."

"All right, that's the point. The difference between socializing today and a couple of decades ago is mind boggling."

I saw what he was driving at. I nodded. "You're talking about e-mail."

"E-mail is just part of it. I'm talking about the whole electronic miracle: E-mail, the Internet, voice mail, chat groups. Twenty years ago I had to rack my brain to call to mind fifteen or 20 friends with whom I maintained more than rare or occasional contact. Today, especially since I sold my business and tapered down to two or three days of work a week, I'm in touch with *hundreds* of friends, many with interests and activities closely related to my own."

I tossed him a look. *"Hundreds!"*

"Maybe more. If you want an example or two, out of many, check out chat groups like ThirdAge or 65Plus on the Internet."

I did. Here's what I learned, quoted right from the Internet.

What Is the ThirdAge

1. A time of life characterized by happiness, freedom and learning.
2. A life stage following "youth" and preceding old age.
3. A Web site where like-minded people find intelligent conversations and useful tools. 4. Your best years ever.

"In my first age," the typical ThirdAger says, "I developed into a person. In my second age, I pursued my career and raised my family. Now, in this ThirdAge of life, I have come into my own. This is my time for creativity, continuous learning, and exploration. I have plenty of energy, plenty of resources, and a fully developed sense of what to do with them. It is my time to enjoy new relationships, appreciate family and friends, and explore the spiritual side of life. It is also my time if I choose, for giving back to society, for sharing the wisdom of my experiences."

What a grand opportunity, I thought, for people with time on their hands to use as many hours as they wish to selectively contact friendly compatible people and exchange thoughts and opinions and develop long-lasting relationships -- people as close by as your own home town, or as far afield as other parts of the world.

ThirdAge goes a giant step beyond random member-to-member chatting. I clicked "community" on its home page, for example, and found the following additional clickable options:

- Postcards to friends
- Voice your opinions
- Free email – keep in touch
- Chat – meet new friends
- Home page – move into your community
- Circles – build your circle of friends

Under community events, I found "Sunday's Schedule" – Who's chatting now?

> 11:00 a.m. – Comparative religion
> 3:00 p.m. – Project Phoenix chat
> 4:00 p.m.– Chronic pain chat
> 5:00 p.m. – ThirdAge chat trivia game
> 6:00 p.m.– Loss and loneliness

I brought up 65Plus on the Internet and learned I was visitor No. 21,732 . Multiply this number by hundreds if not thousands of similar Web sites and you get a rough idea of the popularity of chat groups.

Home Page of 65 Plus
"FOR THE YOUNG AT HEART." Billed as The Friendliest Channel on the Undernet.

With whom do you socialize? Typically, in the "good old days", you met someone at a meeting, organization, or club, and you either hit it off or you didn't. Clearly, you're more likely to be compatible if you share mutual interests. That's why there are Web sites and chat groups for writers, executives, athletes, entertainers, engineers and a long list of specializations covering your local area and the world at large. The Internet covers the globe. You explore at your leisure and select chat candidates who pique your particular interest. If it works out, fine. If not, so long it was nice knowing you. No harm done, and you try again.

The 65Plus Home Page includes a boxed section that features the self-assigned nicknames of such members as – Bert68, DesrtRat, Dunes, Minn-Joe, SalPal, Scots, Zingo, etc. You click on a "nick" and typically, bring up a photo and usually a brief bio as well. For security reasons and to avoid unwanted junk mail, I would assume, actual home addresses and surnames are most commonly omitted. These can be determined later if a contact clicks. At least one "Match Made In Channel 65Plus" – appears to have wound up in marriage. I clicked on a handful of nicks for a rough sampling of 65Plus members.

Minn-Joe – A retired associate computer test engineer, formerly with Xerox in Los Angeles, now residing in Las Vegas. "I never went to college. I am only better than the persons who think they are better than I." Minn-Joe, pictured with his dog, invites visitors to his personal home page or email address.

Goofus – Born 1927 in Colorado, he now resides in Eastern Washington. Twice married, once divorced. Journeyman stereotyper, computer typesetter, Goofus is now semi-retired, works part time in the County's printing department. A Navy vet, he enlisted when he turned 17, served in the Amphibious Corps, completed high school when he returned home in '48. He is also a professional ballroom and square dance instructor.

TNJumper – Veronica "Ronnie", age 49. Born in Newark, NJ. Weighs 135 lbs, (74 lbs. less than 6 months ago). Currently resides in Hanging Limb, Tennessee "where we raise Great Pyrenees dogs and Rheas and Ostriches. An insurance agent, Ronnie's hobbies are genealogy, Internet, word games, knitting and sewing. With 7 children aged 13 to 33, she also serves on the Governor's Council for Developmental Disabilities.

Retee – Age 61, with her husband of 42 years, Retee (which in golf is a "mulligan" or stroke you don't have to count) is a re-**FIRED** grocery store owner. With three children and 4 grandchildren, in addition to golf, she is into gambling, computers, and the study of Spanish.

Burt68 – Born 1923 in Yakima, Washington, he now lives in Bremerton.. A Navy electronic systems inspector for 36 years, and well into the Internet, past hobbies include model airplanes, coin collecting, hotrodding, motorcycle racing, photography and, currently amateur radio.

Interesting people!

This is a miniscule sampling of the tens of thousands of friendly men and women signed up in hundreds of Internet chat groups. Look hard enough and you are sure to find some with whom you would find it enjoyable and informative to establish an electronic -- or more personal -- relationship.

Many, if not most, Internet chat groups go beyond random gabbing into community and special interests. People with problems and special needs relating to health, finances, career options, or whatever, access chat groups to exchange ideas, opinions, and experience. As one chat enthusiast confides, "The chat group is one of the best research tools I know. You accept or reject what you learn, and most often the information you get is offered willingly, and without a commercial ax to grind."

Workers and Drones

Workers are only fulfilled when they keep meaningfully busy – if not full time, at least much of the time. Drones ordinarily don't think in terms of fulfillment. They're happy, or pretend to be content, if unburdened by work commitments. Having survived mid-life, drones reason they have earned the right to "take life easy" from here on out. I have no quarrel with this rationale. Worker or drone, one has every right to spend one's time as one sees fit. Workers and drones, however, have different requirements for contentment. Workers must keep productively occupied – productively, by their own standards and definition – oftentimes on a limited schedule "as the years whittle down to a precious few."

Life becomes less complicated if, at mid-life or thereabouts, you define who you are, worker or drone, and do so as honestly and objectively as possible. If you're a committed drone, convinced that the TV room's couch or poolside chaise is your natural habitat, this section isn't for you. What follows is addressed to the 50+ man or woman who, rather than "throwing in the sponge" at age 60 or so, wants to keep going a decade or three longer, or is interested in exploring other occupational pursuits either full or part time, and either profit or nonprofit based. Unfortunately, an untold number of employed people who -- like Richard Levy described earlier, was faced with the choice of demotion or separation at age 65 -- are not ready to be victimized by that fraudulent number. If you count yourself part of this group, where do you go from here?

Innumerable life renewal alternatives exist. But at this point let's deal specifically with the skilled, productive, and experienced person who in the foreseeable future faces the prospect of being retired or downsized. Time was not so long ago, when an in-danger-of-being-discarded employee in this spot had little recourse but to:

1. Place a job wanted ad in the local paper.
2. Scan local help wanted ads.
3. Call contacts in the field and make your availability known.

4. Contact a recruiter or employment agency.
5. Solicit friends, neighbors, and relatives to be on the outlook for openings.

It is an indisputable fact of the marketplace that the more pipelines a job seeker can open, the more opportunities for connection exist. Well, the good news today is that if one is even moderately computer savvy, pipeline opportunities are expandable from a handful to a multitude. Sometimes for free, sometimes for a moderate charge. If you're not there already, maybe it's time to hop on the bandwagon.

From SeniorNet (www.seniornet.org) "Bringing Wisdom to the Information Age." One of many such Internet resources.

"The nonprofit SeniorNet provides adults 50+ education for and access to computer technology to enhance their lives and enable them to share their knowledge and wisdom."

"SeniorNet is based on the concept that older people are not averse to using new technology, just unfamiliar with it. And once they have access to the new tools and the knowledge of how to use them, technology can enrich their lives.

-- *The Washington Post*

Employment Resources Unlimited

Fact: 76 million baby boomers, most in their forties and 50s are in the job market today as opposed to only 56 million baby busters most in their twenties and 30s.

Reality: Even if the economy's growth slows, there won't be enough workers beginning in the next decade – especially skilled and experienced workers -- to satisfy profit and nonprofit business staffing requirements. Stated more simply, the qualified re-FIRE--ee will be in greater demand than ever before.

From *The Wall Street Journal*: "...**RETIREMENT FOR SOME doesn't mean saying goodbye to work.** Faced with worker shortages, many employers are asking some retirees to stay on as part-timers, consultants, or telecommuters, says Watson Wyatt Worldwide. In a survey of 586 large employers, the New York consulting firm found that 16% offer 'phased retirement,' while 28% say they may set up such programs in the next three years..."

I predict that in much less time than that these figures will be doubled.

The only problem remaining is that of connecting the demanders and demandees. Step one: Define your desire and need. Step two: Access the Internet – on your own, or with the help of a guru – in order to make the connection. What follows is a small sampling of linkage opportunity web sites.

From Working Today: Directory of Resources

The Internet Business Network annually ranks job-search sites. It also provides a daily newsletter and links to 4,000 company web pages.

The Riley Guide is a free service that introduces the novice to the many sites out there and offers links and advice for conducting an Internet job search.

"MBA Free Agents is an online placement service that connects MBAs working as independent contractors with organizations in need of high level talent on a project basis. MBA Free Agents is trying to provide corporate clients with a one-stop resource for finding people who are interested in consulting, sweat-for-equity, and other nontraditional opportunities. The company's service was profiled in the *Wall Street Journal*, Fast Company, and the *Internet World*.

Senior Citizens Job Bureau links seniors who register for regular, part time, or temp work with employers who have job vacancies. Its slogan: "Ability is ageless."

The More Specific, the Better

As any personnel or human resources professional could confirm, specificity is the key in matching "round pegs" to round holes. JobBankUSA (www.jobbankusa.com), invites job seekers to post their resumes to its web site. An up-front fee is paid by the employers for employment advertising and access to the resume data base. What follows is an anonymous posting by one job candidate. How-to-contact instruction for interested employers is included.

Position: Sales Manager/Representative, city, state, and zip, willing to relocate. Years experience: 20+. Salary: $60,000.

Objective: A challenging outside sales position in a growth-oriented organization which offers diverse job responsibilities.

Professional Highlights: Experienced sales specialist in high volume commodity and specialty sales, market development, and sales management. // Proven performance with demonstrated ability to gain account loyalty and win preferential treatment for products. // Excellent rapport building, presentation, and closing skills. // Proven ability to modify product emphasis to match industries and markets serviced. // Strong background encompassing sales, distribution and staff development and motivation.

(Also included: Employers past and present, plus achievements for each, educational profile, and awards received).

Equally detailed and comprehensive are posting by employers in search of specific talents, skills, and experience. An example from Senior Housing Net:

NYC – Senior Business Analyst – up to $85,000

Here is an opportunity to join a leader in the Healthcare industry. This hire will be required to plan and direct analysis of business problems to be solved with automated systems.

Responsibilities:

- Analyze business functions in order to develop new or modified information processing systems.
- Consult with business unit management and personnel to identify and document business needs.
- Research, develop, and write content for printed manuals, documentation and supporting materials for software and

hardware, technical procedures and computer related services.

- Consult and coordinate with systems analysts and programmers to design and develop automated business systems.
- Prepare time and cost estimates for completing projects.

Requirements: Five years related Healthcare or Managed care experience.

Candidates are told whom to contact if interested in exploring this opportunity.

Whether career opportunities are posted by employee or employer, that they are viewed by thousands of people with match making capability makes the potential for successful linkage clear. It's a new world out there. If you are a candidate for forced retirement, downsizing, or job burnout – and still career-minded in your fifties, 60s, or 70s, the Internet could be the best thing that ever happened to you.

Why are people fifty and 60 plus seeking employment? For a variety of reasons. The main reason, surveys report, is financial need. Number two, says Kristin Andersen in *Natural Foods Merchandiser*, is emotional fulfillment. "Older people aren't that concerned about advancement, but they want to enjoy themselves. They value stability and establishing a rapport with coworkers." They also want to get into the mainstream, to feel important, to count.

What kind of work and how much involvement interests you? Part time, flex time, temporary? Whatever your personal need, well worth checking out is AARP's National Older Workers Information System database ("Business Partnerships Program").

Join the senior power parade

Americans have been so brainwashed over the centuries about the superiority of youth over age that, if you are a typical person in your fifties or older, the odds are high that you don't appreciate the immense power you possess in today's economy. Definitions of power in *The American Heritage Dictionary* include: 1. The ability or capacity to perform effectively. 2. A specific capacity, facility, or aptitude. 3. A person, group, or nation having great influence or control over others.

If you are past 50, and that doesn't ring a personal bell, it should. If you are ever plagued by that self-defeating over-the-hill let-down feeling, brighten up. Healthy fifty and over job candidates represent one of the largest and most significant markets in today's economy. That's power. As personnel professionals and consultants almost universally agree, persons fifty and older are the most productive and dependable employees in the marketplace. That's power. People fifty and older are, as a group, more experienced, trained, and knowledgeable than their younger counterparts. That's power. In the ever-tightening labor market of the next decade or two, 50+ veteran employees will be in greater demand than ever. That's power. Those who are the most experienced and most knowledgeable are in the best position to influence others. That's power.

Another critical dimension of power relates to the flexibility and freedom of choice we acquire as we grow older. If we so desire we can change careers, opt for no career at all, or choose to work for money or the thrill, excitement, and fulfillment of the enterprise. We can experiment, take a flyer, pursue a long concealed dream. In decades past, with a family to support and educate and an asset base to develop, many of us were stuck where we were because that's where the job or business happened to be. Today if we wish, for whatever reason we choose, we are free to relocate.

Is the job market tight where you live? Climate too cold? Too much traffic? Too many bad things happening in the area? Have your closest friends and grown-up kids moved away? Are lawn tending and home repairs too much of a bother? Perhaps it's time to change your mindset. Pack up and leave if you and your live-in decide it's what you want to do. What the hell! Who's stopping you?

SPELL OUT WHO YOU ARE AND HOW YOU WANT TO SPEND YOUR TIME

"The life that is unexamined is not worth living."
                                                    Plato

I'm not asking you to sit in judgment of anyone other than yourself. What follows are hypothetical models of what I define as **The 5 Stages of Activity**. Ponder each with the values in mind that are most meaningful to you (love, family, money, spiritual enrichment, cultural development, societal payback, entertainment and fun). Talk it over with your significant other. Then determine if you can which of the following role models you would most want to emulate for the rest of your life.

<u>Stage One</u> – FULL TIME PLUS. **Joel B, age 66.** Insurance company executive. Still averages 60 hours per week despite doctor's caution that he's shortening his life. A workaholic for years, he and his family have long since grown apart. Aside from golf on Sunday and occasional shows, Joel finds little time for recreation, and virtually no time for cultural activity or spiritual fulfillment.

<u>Stage Two</u> – FULL TIME NORMAL. **Mary J, age 57.** Mary enjoys her secretarial job, but is sometimes tweaked by the feeling that five full days a week is getting to be a bit much. Lots of things she would like to do – family things, fun things, charity things, cultural things – that she doesn't seem to find time for. The thought has occurred to her: Maybe it's time she started tapering down.

<u>Stage Three</u> – PART TIME CAREER. **Fred M, age 62.** Fred's a collision specialist and considers him an artist of sorts, auto bodies his canvas. He can make a beat-up fender look better than new, enjoys his craft, but confines his working hours to Tuesday, Wednesday, and Thursday. He and Emma often get away for long weekends, are duplicate bridge aficionados and tennis buffs. Both engage in volunteer work. Emma teaches Sunday school; Fred is on the church board.

<u>Stage Four</u> –HALF VOLUNTEER, HALF STUDENT. **Alice J.,**

60. Alice has two credos she lives by: 1. Never too busy to help others, 2. Never too knowledgeable to learn more. If there's a community job to be done you can count on Alice to pitch in. Between volunteer organizations and the Sisterhood, her phone doesn't stop ringing. Between Elderhostel and local educational opportunities, she is always on the go in her quest for "continuing education."

<u>Stage Five</u> – FULL TIME EASY LIVER. **Charley C.**, 62. Charley plays a lot, sleeps a lot, and watches loads of TV when he's not dozing off. A typical day consists of rising by 10:00 AM or so, followed by a late leisurely breakfast. He recently gave up tennis as too strenuous, but his shuffleboard game hasn't slowed down. Afternoons usually find him on the golf course for nine holes, followed by a gabfest at poolside about "early bird" meals or the stock market. As Charley says, "I worked hard all my life, now I'm having a ball."

Nitty Gritty Time -- Let's get one thing straight. This is your life. Your time is your own. You have every right to use it as you see fit. Thus we make no lofty judgments. Life is a stage. With the years ahead in mind, which stage suits you best -- Joel's, Mary's, Fred's, Alice's, or Charley's. What we are after is *self-assessment*. The verdict is yours alone.

144

Chapter 9
Make Time for Others

Giving back for all you've been getting

"We make a living by what we get; we make a life by what we give."

Anonymous

The businessman I interviewed a month or so ago prefers to remain anonymous. CEO of a large holding company with multi-million dollar enterprises under his control, he conceded that fueling up for renewal sounds like a good idea, but said he's been re-fired all his life. "So long as my health holds out," he added, "I'll be right here at the grindstone doing what I do best and what I love to do most. In fact, if you want to know, I suspect this is what's causing my health to hold out."

At age 76, this spirited dynamic executive couldn't begin to recount the number of million dollar deals he made in his lifetime. "But I can tell you one thing," he said with a chuckle, "No deal I ever made gave me half the joy and satisfaction I derived from helping to fund a center and hospital for mentally retarded kids and serving on its board of directors."

The ultimate recipient

Mohammed said it: "A man's true wealth hereafter is the good that he does in this world to his fellows."

I couldn't tell you how often I have heard this paraphrased by men and women who contribute their time, money, and brain

145

power in an effort to make life easier for people in need. If you believe in the hereafter, no action you take or strategy you devise could be in your better self-interest. There's no question about it. When you are a generous giver, the ultimate beneficiary is you.

Gertrude Weinberg

Wynmoor Village in Coconut Creek, Florida is a so-called "retirement community," inhabited by 9,000+ plus "residents" who are age 55 or older. For a good part of its population, thanks to its cultural, educational, athletic, recreational and group activities, Wynmoor qualifies as a 21st century renewal community. More about this mode of living in the next chapter, but for now Gert Weinberg, one of Wynmoor's most popular and loved residents, should serve as an inspiration for us all.

Gert is not only re-**FIRED** to the hilt herself, but has helped to re-FIRE hundreds of others as well. One might say she is dedicated to the art of rekindlement. Her life has been largely devoted to dancing. She danced professionally in innumerable shows and concert performances, and for a while with New York's famed Roxyettes. She owned a dance studio in Edison, New Jersey, and taught dancing for over 50 years. When she "retired" to Wynmoor over a decade ago, she lost no time setting up a teaching and performance program working with Wynmoor residents mainly in their 60s, 70s, and yes, a handful or so in their 80s. What she has done to professionalize these men and women would have to be seen to be believed. Every other year Gert conceives, directs, and choreographs a revue that packs Wynmoor's spacious theatre at $5.00 a head that would do Broadway proud.

The most recent show as of this writing, "Manhattan Merry Go-Round" was described as "a potpourri of song and dance celebrating the Big Apple". More than a year of weekly rehearsals under Gert's tough demanding directorship has achieved remarkable results: A dance line that rivals the Rockettes, song and dance routines sparked with creativity and fun, emceeing by Stu Addison that would enhance a Broadway stage, plus overture and accompaniment by Wynmoor's very own orchestra. The steady relentless grind proves too much for some; there have been dropouts. But most survive and flourish in the glory and pride of achievement that follows. Shows are performed not only at Wynmoor, but in theatres all over South Florida. Gert also serves on the board of the Area Agency on Aging and has been elected to Broward County's Senior Hall of Fame. Her troupe's performances have raised over $100,000 for local senior facilities.

I can think of no more persuasive example for the joys and rewards of gutsy renewal than Gert Weinberg. What a contrast between Gert and all too many of her counterparts who mope around bemoaning the aging process with its accompanying aches and pains and centering their lives around poolside schmoozing about "early bird" meals and investments!

Why enrich your life with volunteer and other activity-based programs as the years whittle down? At no time in one's life does the answer become more apparent than when a loved one dies as did Gert's husband two years ago. Being Gert , she had neither the time nor inclination to prolong grieving beyond its normal and natural phase. She keeps too busy giving and doing. In her spare time (hah-hah) she paints and sculpts. An avid golfer, she is vice president of the Ladies Golf Association at Wynmoor. She organized and served as president of the complex's well attended Cultural Club. She serves as president of her condo, Nassau West 2, and oversees six buildings.

I asked her, "Don't you ever get pressed for time?" Gert's answer: "Never."

I also asked "Why? Why do you do it; what do you get out of it?"

She smiled. "Two things. First and foremost, I do it for myself, because I love it. Secondarily, because I enjoy helping people."

It's well worth repeating: *The ultimate beneficiary is you!*

How much giving can you afford?

The payback responsibility should rightfully nag the conscience of every person whose lifetime yielded success, health, and happiness. Some give back for what they get in a straightforward manner, endowing hospitals or colleges, sponsoring programs to relieve poverty or provide educational opportunities for young people and minorities, or to reduce hunger and despair in oppressed and undeveloped third world countries. Others respond to the beat of their own inner drummers.

"When it comes to giving away money," *People Magazine* writes, "Alan Ginsberg, chairman of Bear, Stearns & Co., has a penchant for the unconventional. 'You made your money,' his wife Kathryn told him, 'you can spend it in any way you want.'"

Greenberg, 72, whose annual income exceeds $20 million, has doled out millions for causes ranging from renovation of the bathrooms of Jerusalem's Israel Museum to endowing a skeletal dyslexia center at Johns Hopkins Hospital. His objective is to help others where he perceives help is needed instead of just accumulating cash. One donation, after seeing insurers balk at picking up the tab, was a million dollars to New York City's Hospital for Special Surgery to fund Viagra prescriptions for financially needy impotent men. Some question the largesse. But as Kathryn says, "It's his money."

> How careful we are about how we handle our money.
> Are we as careful about investing our time? Time is
> our most valuable asset, it is worth far more than
> time which we safeguard so carefully.
>
> Dr. Paul Parker

Queen Elizabeth said on her death bed: "All my possessions for a moment of time."

God gave us the gift of time to use wisely or squander. **Wisely** includes such uses as earning and learning, health-sustaining exercise, interaction with friends and family, help for others less fortunate than ourselves, reading, travel, recreation and athletic activity we really and truly enjoy, bridge or other card games that stimulate and relax us. The goal is to keep productively occupied. Or we're free to **squander** our time with such no-win pursuits as boring and meaningless poolside or telephone chit chat, exchanging "early bird" dining alternatives, or suffering through the glut of television's deadly fare.

My theory regarding God's precious gift is simple: THE MORE TIME WE SPEND PRODUCTIVELY, THE LESS TIME WE WILL HAVE AVAILABLE TO SPEND **WORRYING** ABOUT OUR HEALTH OR FINANCES, ENTERTAINING **FEARS** RELATED TO OUR LOVED ONES AND JOBS, OR **ANXIOUSLY** PONDERING THE SAD STATE OF WORLD CONDITIONS WITH THE DEVASTATING MENTAL AND PHYSICAL HEALTH CONSEQUENCES OF AGGRAVATION ANDANXIETY.

Len And Ethel Smith

South Florida's Leonard J. Smith is the consummate teacher. His wife Ethel is the consummate doer. Both qualify as ideal evidentiary models of my time theory as expressed above. Each has his fair share of physical ailments, but neither has the time or patience to allow themselves to slow down. Len is only 82, but a scan-down of his bio would seem to cover two centuries, careers overlapping of course, though as Len insists, he doesn't look a day over 80.

- 18 years as an executive in the lighting and lingerie industries.
- 42 years as an adjunct professor at Rutgers University, NYU, Manhattan College, Fairleigh Dickenson, and the University of Wisconsin.

- 38 years as a management consultant.
- Founder and President of New Jersey's Training Services, Inc. (TSI)
- A founder of the American Society of Personnel Administrators. Now known as the Society of Human Resource Management (SHRM).
- Author of 5 textbooks on labor relations and career planning.
- Following TSI's sale to the Center for Professional Advancement, Len served for three years as a vice president of this organization.
- Longstanding member of the American Arbitration Association called upon to settle countless labor disputes.
- Still active as a consulting editor for Personnel Policy Services, Inc. in Louisville, Kentucky.

Ethel, 85, had a long and diversified career in management, operating and selling apartment buildings, shopping centers, and apartment complexes.

Payback time for the Smiths dates back decades as does their renewal decisions. Though "well fixed," their financial and material assets fall far short of the billion dollar mark. Nonetheless, the Leonard & Ethel Smith Charitable Foundation, a nonprofit organization, makes generous annual contributions to causes ranging from education and research to Judaic charities in America and Israel.

Len, who with all his awards could open a trophy shop, serves on numerous boards in the U.S. and Israel. A sampling: He is on the boards of three Israeli universities: the American Association for the Weizman Institute, the American Association for Ben Gurion University, and Bar Ilon University, where he is active in planning, organization, and fund raising. He also serves on the board of the American Association for Israeli Disabled War Veterans.

Len finds time too – when he doesn't find it, he *makes* it – to serve as financial secretary of his temple, president of the Men's Club, and Head of Security for his condo development. (When someone begs off involvement because they don't have the time, he believes, it's a copout.)

Ailments? Len has his share. He hobbles around with a cane. "It goes with the territory," Len says with a grin. Ethel too, is no stranger to medical facilities. Yet they both "work out" at least an hour each day.

Busy? That's not the half of it. A large chunk of the Smiths' time these days is devoted to South Florida's network of Prostate Cancer Support Groups which is now nationwide. Founded by Len in 1990, following his own bout with the illness, he is now a regional coordinator. Working with hospitals, doctors, research scientists, and the American Cancer Society, he plans and organizes meetings, serves as speaker, fills in for doctors and other specialists whose patient commitments prevent them from showing up, and coordinates activities for 19 South Florida groups. Ethel is right there at his side at meetings, serving as secretary and, as a follow-up of her lifelong career skills, managing seating, hosting, food dispensation, and other aspects.

Len's favorite story doesn't deal with any of this. What it involves is the time he hit a home run in the Yankee Stadium. More years ago than he cares to remember, he was a pitcher with the Kiwanis League which played a benefit game at the Stadium against the Frankie Darrow League. In the third inning, he thinks it was, "I got lucky. It was probably a bad pitch." But wham! When the slider crossed the plate, Len gave it everything he had and the ball soared over right field into the stands.

What the Smiths give to others – of their time and money, and most of all of themselves -- is clear. But again the key question is *Why*? What do they get out of it? One thing is obvious; many, perhaps most folks of their age and state of health would, without their determination to fight the ravages of the downside of age, be confined to wheelchairs, bedridden, or worse. Not this pair! As Ethel puts it, "We don't have the time for that nonsense."

Len says reflectively, "I'm a teacher. Almost all of my life I've been devoted to teaching. I love it. I'll never stop. It keeps me young."

When one looks beyond money and its material byproducts, the insight can achieve dimensions both uplifting and inspirational.

Microsoft employee Trish Millines made big bucks from Microsoft options. But for her it wasn't enough and I'm not talking about money. She reasoned: How much do you really need to live comfortably and derive joy and satisfaction from life? Her inner drummer responded that so far as wealth is concerned, enough is enough. She quit her job, *Newsweek* reports, and founded a foundation to teach tech to inner-city kids. "The money basically fell in my lap," she says. "I wanted to do something with it besides collect houses and cars." As folks like Millines will confirm, the rewards of giving far exceed the rewards of getting.

As a society we've been psyched into equating giving with making financial donations to "worthwhile causes." The need for money, of course, cannot be over-stressed. Causes require funding to stay operational and survive .

But what if you're not one of the privileged few? Six out of 10 boomers, reports Knight-Ridder writer Kay Harvey, – the glut of Americans born between 1946 and 1964 – have no idea how much savings they will need to support themselves when the paychecks stop coming, let alone contribute to others, according to a study commissioned for mutual-fund companies Fidelity and Scudder. "If you can't put 10 percent of your paycheck away," says investment broker Rand Winspear, "you're missing out on why you're going to work."

But what if you're 50 or 60 and lacked the foresight to bank that ten percent, or lacked the ten percent for the banking? What if at this point in your life you can't afford to donate millions, or even thousands or hundreds, to worthwhile causes? Does that mean you will be left out in the cold when you stand worried and apprehensive at the Hereafter Judgment Gate waiting for Pete's nod of admission? Not at all. Not if, like Gert Weinberg, the Smiths, and countless others, your payback responsibility battery has been morally charged. In any number of cases I could cite, a sacrifice on a par with if not greater than the gift of money is the gift of oneself – one's love, one's time.

Givers Most Blessed

How much money do you need to fulfill your payback responsibility for blessings received and indeed, survival itself, in a perilous and uncertain world? Very little, maybe just enough for bare sustenance.

Martha, 62, a former English teacher, recalls the days when her financial assets could be stated in five figures. That's no longer the case. She can't afford to donate money, but devotes hours each week to upgrading reading and writing skills of Black and Latino teenagers,

Overlook the irony of her name. Arlene Rich, 58, who is on food stamps, leads a big band that plays freebee dances at senior centers and nursing homes.

Marvin Miller, 53, had a drastic change of heart – and outlook – when his Internet investment strategy resulted in an $87,000 loss and left him dead broke. "It caused me to review and reevaluate my goals," Miller says, "and I don't mean my financial goals alone. Life has been damned good to me. Wonderful wife. Exceptional children. Three beautiful grandkids. I figure it's well past time that I should start to pay back." Miller, a self-employed accountant, participates in a program that provides transportation for the elderly and infirm. On Sunday he conducts Bible classes in his church.

Good government doesn't happen automatically. You have to get out there in your community and become involved to make it occur. So believes Robert Spector who retired after 11 years as a New York City firefighter. Now 81, he doesn't have big bucks to contribute, but he does have big time. Bob worked hard with the help of local office holders to organize a nonpartisan, multiracial, Democratic club and keep it operational. His dedicated goal is to get out the vote. "I make a difference," he says with a glow.

Two years ago, the *Wall Street Journal* reports, Veda Ponikvar of Chisholm, Minnesota, sold the two weekly newspapers she owned and no longer has to worry about meeting payrolls and filling out government forms. Now, at 78, she devotes her time to serving on the boards of civic groups, charting the history of immigrants, and working with the mentally retarded. She has never been happier.

People over 50, according to a study by the Alliance for Aging Research, "are seen as far more generous and less self-centered than those under 50." The conclusion is clear: Giving is a sign of maturity.

Rose Garfinkel

Feisty, independent Rose, 83, won't reveal her bank account balance. But, says her daughter Sheila, "you can bet it's on the short side of four figures."

The records do show she has logged over 30 thousand hours of volunteer service in Liberty, New York's Community General Hospital. "I don't know what I'd do without her," says Peter Notarstefano, director of the hospital's Volunteer Service.

For *decades* Rose has served whenever and wherever she was needed: At the information desk, at the Baby Fair for expectant mothers, boosting the morale of patients without visitors, arranging late snacks for the detox unit, working with staff editors, assisting with arts and crafts, running bingo games, helping with the administration of food programs, as a replacement for absentee volunteers, pushing a food cart three times her size all over the hospital. No task is beneath Rose's dignity, too dirty, or too much of a challenge to her sensitivity and compassion. She patiently feeds severely aging and difficult patients. She spends hours reading to poor-sighted patients, comforting the depressed and dispirited. Seven days a week she is on an eight or nine hour schedule.

"Oh yes," one nurse concedes, "we have a capable hardworking administration, and several important doctors on staff. But from a down-to-earth human and humane perspective, Rose runs the hospital."

Once, when Rose was a patient herself, she continued to volunteer from her bed, organizing meal tickets, comforting other patients, and handling a variety of paperwork.

RSVP Senior of the Year for the town of Liberty, she proudly showed me her scrapbook, which runs for pages and pages. *Why, Rose? What motivates this kind of dedication?* Well, for one thing, she has had several bouts with serious illness herself. She understands how patients feel and is sensitive to their needs from personal experience. But when I asked her these questions she echoed Gert Weinberg's sentiments. "It's for *me*. I love it. It makes me feel like I'm *somebody*. After all, what would I be if I wasn't doing this work?"

Give while you're still working

Make time for others while you're still employed and the inevitable payoff is that you will make time for yourself. I know from long personal experience how powerful and rewarding this concept can be.

The benefits stem from face-to-face involvement and interaction. I couldn't begin to recall how many universities, charitable, cultural, and other nonprofit organizations I served on over the years as both business owner and employee, as board member and in other capacities. Nor could I begin to recall the payoff from this service in terms of contacts made and opportunity gates opened as well as useful experience and the chance to polish talents and abilities.

Face it. The more people you know, the more good shots you will have when:

- You need a job.
- You need to hire an employee with specialized skills and experience.
- You have something to sell.
- You have a fundraising obligation to meet.
- You need allies to support and assist you in bringing a dream or idea to fruition.
- You need an introduction or lead to someone who can help you.

The more you interact with people the better exposure you will get for your talents, abilities and experience. It's amazing too what involvement with others, speaking before groups, promoting causes face-to-face and the like, can do to overcome shyness, spark personality, and build confidence. You will also increase the number of lists you will be on for access when others need what you have to offer. You will not only have a wider population to call upon when presented with a need; others will come to you when they have their own needs to fulfill. My current job as marketing vice president of Lynn University derived as a direct consequence of my community interaction and involvement with dozens of boards, programs, and other activities.

Observes Kathy Scott, special events coordinator for the Chamber of Commerce of Florida's Palm Beaches, "When you get involved organizing an Offshore Grand P:rix or Firefighter of the Year event, you begin working together with others. As people get to know and like you, they will do business with you – and refer you to people they know. At one chamber lunch," she adds, "three of the 10 attendees earned new business because they came to give, rather than take."

It's the way life works. What you do for others, you do most of all for yourself, psychologically, spiritually, and materially.
Like all other worthwhile activities, the most effective and efficient giving is the giving you plan wisely and thoughtfully. The more intensely the cause or program you become involved with touches your mind and your heart, the more value the recipient – and you as the co-beneficiary -- will derive from your gift of money or time. From the list below tick off the causes and human needs that move you most. Consider this sampling as a platform from which to launch your efforts.

1. American families below the poverty level   ____
2. Starvation in third world countries   ____
3. Gun ownership – for or against   ____
4. Abortion – Choice or Right to Life   ____
5. Educational opportunities for minorities   ____
6. Organizations fighting racial intolerance   ____

7. Support for culture and the arts   ____
8. Peace in our time   ____
9. Retarded or otherwise afflicted children   ____
10. Nuclear proliferation   ____
11. Aid for unwed mothers   ____
12. Parents who welsh on support   ____
13. TV and film violence   ____
14. HMO abuses   ____
15. War on drugs   ____
16. Escalating drug and medical costs   ____
17. Special interest groups   ____
18. Parents without partners   ____
19. Pornography on the Internet   ____
20. Clean environment   ____
21. Religious freedom   ____
22. Campaign reform   ____
23. Getting out the vote   ____
24. Transportation for the elderly   ____
25. Minimum wage   ____
26. Equality in the workplace   ____
27. Political party of your choice   ____
28. Sex education   ____
29. Campaign reform   ____
30. Burgeoning world population   ____
31. Global warming   ____
32. Flood and other catastrophic relief   ____

As you can see, there is no shortage of human suffering and human need. Select the cause or causes that move you most, and you will derive maximum satisfaction and joy from your giving.

Painless Giving

What a great idea! Say your intentions are good. You *want* to fulfill you payback debt obligation. But you want to have a good time while doing it. Why not? Who can argue with multiple mileage? So you love to travel, and maybe you recall reading Paulette Thomas's fine article, "Giving Back," some time ago in the *Wall Street Journal*. Subtitled, "Volunteer vacations let people explore the world while helping others." And the thought settles in and begins to intrigue you. The more you ponder it, the more you wonder, "Could this be for me?"

It might be if you're provoked by Boca Raton, Florida's Sanford Alberts's experience as a team leader for Global Volunteers, a private, nonprofit organization. Alberts completed a three-week stint in Jeruk Legi, a remote village in Java, Indonesia," writes Thomas, "where he spent mornings teaching English to schoolchildren and afternoons repairing desks and painting walls. Nights were spent of straw mattresses."

At age 67 it was an exciting learning and doing experience. Echoing the song Alberts taught them in the schoolyard gazebo, children called him "Old MacDonald when they passed him on the street. He savored the spicy unfamiliar food, the walks in the mountains, and most of all the relationships cemented. "That's what life is all about, he says. It was all very gratifying."

Adventure travel is booming, and hitched right on to the boom are such volunteer travel groups as Global Volunteers, Earthwatch Institute and Habitat for Humanity, along with many religious organizations and nonprofit groups. Increasingly seniors, and many others not so senior – "volunteer foot soldiers" as they are sometimes referred to – opt for paying their own way abroad to help others as an alternative to packaged cruises and the like. "What's more," says one volunteer, "it winds up costing much less; at least that was my experience."

Global Volunteers in St. Paul, Minn., Thomas reports, "was founded in 1984 by Burnham Philbrook, a 51-year old lawyer and former state legislator, and his wife Michele Gran, 43. The spark for the idea was their honeymoon on an economic-development project in Guatemala. 'We were characterized as hippie holdovers, Ms. Gran recalls. 'People thought we were trying to overthrow governments'." All they wanted was to promote peace and good works. About a third of the volunteers are former teachers, Thomas writes. Especially needed are teachers of English. Myrtle Engebretson-Hutchins, who began taking Global Volunteer treks after her husband died in 1992, now in her 90s, has taught English in Poland, Spain and Italy. If the option intrigues you as it does me, pick up a book by Bill McMillon titled "Volunteer Vacations."

Companies Hopping on the Volunteer Bandwagon

"It's a new world, Goldie," as Tevya remarked in *Fiddler on the Roof*. Fact of Life No. 1: 60 to 65 or thereabouts is now middle-age. Fact of Life No. 2: The number of adults at so-called retirement age is mind-boggling. Smart corporate personnel and human relations executives increasingly view this talent and experience endowed army as potential assets, reports Russel Gerbman in HR Magazine (published by the Society of Human Relations Management – SHRM). Ideal candidates as volunteers and ambassadors for civic and social programs, more and more corporations are waking up to their value.

The National Retiree Volunteer Coalition (NRVC) in Minneapolis, founded in 1977, has helped create about 100 corporate programs for businesses, health care systems, universities and municipalities in 19 states and Canada. A sampling of comments as reported by Gerbman:

Duke Energy Corp. – "...everyone wins – the community has experienced, dedicated volunteers; the retiree feels a sense of value to the company and the community; and the company gets recognition as a good corporate citizen."

Hewlett-Packard – "The retirees help achieve some of the company's own community goals and offer tremendous public relations." Prudential Insurance Co. -- "We hope to have satisfied employees, so we want to have satisfied retirees as well. It's a win, win, win situation."

What kind of programs do retiree volunteers engage in? Typically, food banks, local hospitals, vocational training centers, collecting blankets and coats for the needy, educational programs for teens, homeless shelters, Meals on Wheels, etc.

How are the programs selected? With sensitivity and care, experience shows.

"Volunteers must find the causes they believe are important, worthwhile and interesting," says NRVC's Donna Anderson. "If not, they will walk."

Lucky you

Ten years ago on a cold February morning, New York City bank teller Joel Ellison and his wife Ellen, a research assistant, were hit hard by the news that Joel's dad, a widower, had been killed in an automobile accident. In their 40s at the time, their grief was barely assuaged at the time by a call from his father's lawyer informing them of a $235,000 inheritance. In time, however, after a respectable mourning period, they put their windfall to use.

They did this in grand fashion. And why not, they rationalized? All of a sudden they were *rich*! Prior to the inheritance, with the kids' dental work, mortgage payments, and other expenses, they were scraping by on a bank account of about $30,000.

Joel wangled an extra week's vacation – Ellen quit her job which she hated – and they signed up for a three week trip to the Orient. On their return home they bought a luxury model car, did extensive refurnishing, joined a country club, and lived high on the hog, dining in expensive restaurants and treating themselves to weekend jaunts. By the end of the year, their bank balance was $59,000. They weren't in bad financial shape at the time, but today they don't have the money to pay for the children's college education. They are putting off re-doing the roof because they can't afford it. And with Medicare eligibility a way off, medical bills and drugs are "killing them" almost as much as their ailments.

"Delusions of wealth," columnist Jane Bryant Quinn writes, quoting Harold Evensky of Evensky, Brown & Katz in Coral Gables, Florida. "People often have unrealistic ideas of how much 'big money' is, or how far their inheritance will carry them. They might quit their jobs or jump to a wealthier mode of life, then discover they can't sustain themselves."

Lucky you? If you're fortunate enough to inherit money, what's the best approach to take? First of all, go slow. Don't plunge. If you want some fast fun, experts advise, blow 5 percent of the money, but conserve the rest. As in all of life and business, planning is the key to success. If your windfall is significant, good planning is doubly important, with your kids' education and the future in mind. As well as folks less fortunate than yourself when payback time is at hand.

Chapter 10
Call Your Own Shots

Showing people who is in charge

" How you account to others is less important than how you account to yourself."

Emily Davis

Boisterous, jovial, lovable, stroke-handicapped George Nadler, 70+, a Hungarian-American resident of Wynmoor Village in Coconut Creek, Florida, loves duplicate bridge. He plays the game about ten times a week. He loves his wife, he loves his family, in fact, he loves everyone, and everyone loves him. But one could almost say George's is addicted to this fascinating game which he plays extremely well. Typically, at Wynmoor, a duplicate session involves 40 tables with four players at each table. One-hundred-and-sixty bridge players. George knows them all and they know him. For him bridge is more than a contest or game, it's a social event, and there's no bigger kidder or joker than George.

So what are you gonna tell him? "Cut down. You're wasting away the best years of your life. Devote your time to culture and learning." I would advise strongly against it. He would bite your head off, and rightly so. How George spends his time is his business alone. You can present other options for his consideration. But to be judgmental would be wrong. He has every right to call his own shots, and he is damned well going to do it.

Differentiate between recreation and wreck-reation

New Year's Eve is a time of the year when millions of people venture forth like Knights of the Round Table determined to have a good time, even if it kills them. They put on daffy hats, blow silly horns, rattle tinny noise makers, make an ear-splitting racket, get sick and dopey from too much booze, and try to convince one another they are having a ball ushering in the New Year. More often than not they are putting on an act whether they admit it or not, conning themselves into believing that *wreck*reation is recreation.

With all due respect, the new year should be celebrated, if for no other reason than to offer hope and a prayer that next year will be better, more peaceful, less violent. But from what I have seen, thoughtful and sober celebrants enjoy the experience more than their defiantly merry counterparts. Most people I know, especially those with the gray mixing in, tend to get bleary-eyed by the time the ball falls at Times Square. I couldn't count how many have confessed to me they are relieved when it's over.

Level With Yourself

To paraphrase Lincoln, you can fool all of the people some of the time, and some of the people all of the time. But when you fool yourself you risk fooling around with your lifestyle. As a case in point, consider Lil Goldwyn. Lil has a problem she finds embarrassing. Thursday night is tinkle gin rummy time with "the girls". Since the stakes are "$2.00 pie," it's a serious game, sometimes to the point of being grim. Lil's problem is certainly grim. On occasion she falls asleep *while playing the game.* "Lil, it's your turn." "Er, uh, what?" So this is something to probe. She's only 58, a long way from senility. Was the game so exciting that the stress produced mental fatigue. Or was it simply *out and out boring*? I think you know the answer. So would Lil if she pondered her true feelings. It's one of my biggest problems when I try to help people: How to hammer across the importance of leveling with oneself?

America is a nation of doggedly determined individuals. Counsel that applies to Harry has little application for Frank; an option beneficial to Mary may be detrimental to Jane.

Consider Charley and Joe. Spending an evening at home, Charley tuned in the TV at 8:00 PM to a program called "Buffy the Vampire Slayer." It took him no more than three minutes to give up in disgust and irritatingly change the channel. Wall to wall boredom. Joe, on the other hand, watched the same program. Next day in his black and yellow swim suit, he asked poolside buddies, "Did you catch 'Buffy…' last night? It was hilarious. I laughed my head off."

So, as they say, different strokes for different folks. The strokes you choose are your business and nobody else's. But in evaluating those strokes the smartest move you could make is to level with yourself and respond accordingly regardless of what others might think. Showing the world who's in charge is not only smart. It's the American way.

On the other hand...

Yeah, on the other hand. Let's talk about that old bugaboo, AGE. Too old for what? Horace Mann wrote: "Habit is a cable. We weave a thread of it every day until it becomes so strong we cannot break it." Senior potential aside, most people, as they grow older, unless something stirs them enough to get their brain wheels spinning, are likely to become creatures of habit.

Thus an effort to break George Nadler's duplicate bridge habit would have as much chance of success as persuading Trent Lott to host a Democratic fund-raiser.

But suppose, just suppose, you could have reached some of these habit-bound creatures in their 60s and 70s a decade or so back in their 50s with a menu of new and stimulating options. Who knows how it might have affected their lifestyle today? So, striving not to be judgmental regarding life's choices that turn me off personally, my job here is to present options to readers who are not yet irretrievably habit-bound, that might enrich their lives in years to come. The objective, of course, is to stimulate excitement and interest, promulgate diversity, and thus defeat Killer Boredom.

Are You Too Habit-Bound To Diversify?

Funny thing about boredom which Saul Bellow defines as "the shriek of unused capacities." Ask ten people if they feel their existence boring, at least nine will say no. People are reluctant to admit – to themselves or to others – that they are bored. Dr. George O'Reilly, a psychologist, explains why.

"I know a woman, age 64, whom I'll refer to as Arlene. From my personal perspective, Arlene lives the most boring life I could imagine. Large chunks of her precious time are spent playing Bingo, lounging at poolside discussing "early bird" menus or, if not at poolside on the telephone. In her apartment the TV is tuned to a soap opera. Her husband, 66, naps most of the day when he's not playing cards. Asked if she enjoys her retirement, Arlene defiantly replies she most certainly does. Sobeit! It's her life, her time. Who am I to dispute her assertion?

"Admitting being bored is a threat to one's lifestyle, an implication of stupidity. If you're bored, why not alter the situation or resistance to change that produces the boredom?" Since boredom is self-inflicted, O'Reilly adds, "pretty much the same process that caused it can be used to reverse the condition."

New Jersey customer service supervisor Ben Golden, 55, and his wife Louise offer a prime case in point. For more months than they care to remember, the Golden's have been dining out almost every Friday evening with their next door neighbors, the Bentleys. When they return from the restaurant, they go to one apartment or the other, kibitz for an hour or so, and then play Canasta.

Canasta is a card game that appeals to some, but the Goldens find it boring. They are bright and informed people, no indictment against the game. Many smart people find it relaxing and fun, a viable social activity. The Goldens once enjoyed the game, but as

166

time passed they grew tired of it. Even more boring to them than the game itself are the Bentleys themselves. They rant on interminably about their fabulously successful children with their expensive homes, boats and cars. When this subject -- as well as their neighbors -- are exhausted, Joe Bentley usually turns to his investment triumphs, or Alice to her cooking prowess.

At evening's end, the Goldens are tight and irritable. "Deadly!" Ben grumbles, "why the hell do we put up with it?"

Louise frowns. She agrees. Conflicting emotions, guilt and aggravation, play a duet on her face. "How can we not put up with it?" she says. "They're our neighbors. How can we tell them we don't want to socialize with them any more?"

Ben and Louise shake their heads, see no easy solution.

Are they "good guys," or schmoes? If I could sit this couple down, I might suggest a solution, maybe not so easy, but in my view essential. *"Call your own shots,"* I would say. "Time is God's most precious gift. Your responsibility to yourself is to use it wisely. At the moment you are squandering one evening each week, a substantial part of God's gift."

Boredom imprisons the soul. Given the gumption and will there is no boring situation where a jail break in unachievable. With this thought in mind, let's try an experiment. Compile a list of time expenditures you repeatedly indulge in day after day, week after week. If you're employed, include the job on your list. Eliminate such necessary and unavoidable tasks as wash-up, showers, shaving, and the like. Next, construct a Boredom Index and on a scale of 1 – 5, rate each of these time consumers, with 1 as the least boring and 5 *as the most boring and nonproductive*. What follows is a sampling of items that might be included. Using this as a guideline, compile your own list and make your personal individualized evaluation.

- Work time on the job. _____
- Your lunch period. _____
- Reading time. _____

TV watching. (Break this down into segments)
- Program A _____
- Program B, etc. _____

Recreation and relaxation. (Break down)
- Golf _____
- Tennis _____
- Card games (each specified) etc. _____
- Socializing with friends. _____
- Time spent with family (Break down by members) _____
- Poolside gabbing. _____
- Telephone chit chat. _____
- Daytime naps. _____
- Sleep time. _____
- Travel (Break down by place and activity) _____
- Time spent reading the daily newspaper. _____

Do you get the drift? Build your own list. Be sure to include all repetitive significant time segments. In your 1 – 5 ratings, take care to include *productivity* as a major factor. For example, you may find telephone calls to a parent boring. But since they are important and necessary obligations – unlike time spent with a dull neighbor – it probably warrants a 1 rating. This analysis can help you get more fun and satisfaction from your life whether you are 50 or 70. The follow-up will open your mind to all kinds of opportunities. Ponder the time expenditures on your list that you rated most boring and nonproductive as *you yourself, not others, define them.* Then ponder alternative courses of action designed to minimize, eliminate, or turn the negatives into positives in a way that will enhance and enrich your lifestyle.

I can think of no better example of this experiment's value than Frank Oliphant, 55, a South Florida new car salesman and friend of the family. I suggested the idea to Frank during a lunch date at a local diner after he complained that life's "deadly dull repetition" was causing him to "climb the walls." Adopting a What-do-I-have-to-lose? attitude, he decided to give it a try.

His revelations were intriguing, his follow-up action even more so. Tops on his Boredom Index was his job. He hated the repetitious work and the pressure even more. Other 5's on his list included exercise, specific TV programs, his weekly poker game with guys he didn't really care for, and weekend time spent at poolside. Once an enthusiastic Floridian, global warming had turned him off on South Florida.

So what did he do about it? Frank, a widower, considers himself a "man of action" and proved it. I recently received a phone call from him. He relocated to California and, in partnership with an old school buddy, purchased a new car dealership. He now spends only a fraction of his time on the selling end of the business. A heart patient, Frank's cardiologist prohibits such strenuous activity as tennis or handball. However, somewhat overweight, he understands the importance of exercise that he previously confined to walking which, however beneficial, he finds boring. Today Frank still walks. But he has switched to a treadmill and listens to tapes while he does it. He also does laps in the pool which he finds less boring than walking.

He gave up the weekly poker games, then decided he misses them. Today he is trying to get into a game with a group of men he finds more compatible. TV programs? Aside from Monday night football which he enjoys, he replaced the boring stuff with reading and other activities. Poolside schmoozing has been all but eliminated.

How does all this enhance his existence? "I couldn't begin to tell you," Frank replies. He says he plans to send me a case of booze. I haven't received it yet.

Define busy as you, not others, view it

It would be hard to argue the point that keeping busy is a viable antidote to dissatisfaction in general and boredom in particular. But busy doing what? As Shakespeare said, that's the rub. Individuals that we are, one person's 'busy' is another person's waste of time. We're all too familiar with so-called "busy work," tasks palmed off on the kids, for example, to get them out of our hair. Or work handed to employees that is of little if any value, simply to keep them "occupied" when there's no real work on hand. Unfortunately, phony or sham busy-ness doesn't cut it. You may be able to fight fire with fire. But fighting boredom with boredom never was and never will be a viable option. It tends to backfire. So what it boils down to is that the final arbiter is YOU. It is up to you to determine the kind of busy-ness to inject into your life that will make it more interesting, exciting, and productive. Let's consider some options.

The Fun and Games People

It's not for me, and it may not be for you. But whoever it is for has the right to seize every moment of it for what they get out of it, or what they believe they get out of it. And who is to say they are wrong?

Bruce and Ellie Gruener

The Grueners, Georgia residents aged 62 and 61 respectively, have a great deal going for them. Bruce is a former traffic supervisor in a paper products distributing company. Ellie was also employed by the same firm as a word processing operator. Married for 22 years and comfortably fixed financially, they opted simultaneously for early retirement two years ago. As Ellie spiritedly puts it, "We've been having a ball ever since". Here are some vital background statistics for whatever bearing they may have on the point I am trying to make.

- The Grueners are a compatible couple and very much in love.
- It is a second marriage for both of them.
- Bruce's prior marriage was unhappy and ended in divorce.
- Ellie had a good first marriage. Her husband died of a heart

attack at age 40, leaving her heartbroken for years until she started dating Bruce who is a loving sensitive husband.

- Employed as a supervisor, Bruce disliked his job, didn't get along with his boss, and has dreamed for years of retirement.
- Ellie was not as passionately a job hater as Bruce, but found work boring, boring, boring.
- The Gruens are friendly, sociable people, and have many friends.
- They live in a suburb of Atlanta with a great variety of recreational facilities.

Ellie is the couple's "social secretary." She carries around a calendar memo book that has an entry for almost every day of the month. They enjoy eating out, go to occasional movies, haven't attended a concert in months, and shy away from cultural events. Both say they like to read books, but don't have the time. *They're too busy enjoying themselves.*

The Gruens are fun and games people. Both play tennis. He has his regular games; she has hers. Once a week they play mixed doubles. Both are golfers and hit the links at least twice a week. Most evenings are spent playing table games. Ellie plays mah jong; Bruce enjoys pinochle. Both play gin rummy. They spend several hours each week in the pool or at poolside. They do laps for exercise. Some people who emerge into retirement from a longtime hated job are so relieved to be free of it they are content to play and "relax" for the rest of their lives. The Gruens' faces light up with enthusiasm when asked about the life they lead and the prospects the future holds for them. They are not religious people, but thank God for their good health which enables them to have such a joyous and rewarding existence. "We paid our dues," they say. "Now it's our turn to have a good time."

Personally, I feel my mind would atrophy if I were condemned to such an existence. But who am I to deny the Gruens their turn?

The Perpetual Learners

"Thinking is the hardest work there is, which is the probable reason so few engage in it."

Henry Ford

"I think, therefore I am." Whether articulated or not, a growing number of people are motivated by the conviction to make "continuous education" a major renewal option upon reaching the stage of their life when they gain the flexibility to pursue learning opportunities.

Ford regarded education as his personal fountain of youth, the be-all and end-all of successful fulfillment. He maintained that, "Anyone who stops learning is old, whether at twenty or eighty. Anyone who keeps learning stays young. The greatest thing in life is to keep your mind young."

To which I say *Bravo!* although the Gruens, as is their privilege, might disagree. Millions of others do agree. If you are interested in signing up for this mind-centered club, my suggestion is to get your application in early or, more specifically, investigate the options and plan to take advantages of the ones most appealing to you.

Elderhostel

Elderhostel ("Adventures in Lifelong Learning"), headquartered at 75 Federal Street, Boston, MA 02110-1941, is by all odds the most popular and extensively accessed educational opportunity for people 55 and over. Programs, typically but not consistently, include 3 one-and-a-half hour courses conducted five or 6 days a week. They are held at colleges, learning centers, and other institutions throughout the U.S. and all over the world. Again typically, program tuition runs from about $400 to $600 per person as of this writing, although costs have been rising each year. Fee includes housing in either private rooms with bath, or dorms with toilet and shower down the hall, and meals – usually more than adequate -- in the school cafeteria.

Asked why he enjoyed Elderhostel, Dr. Paul Boyer, a Nobel Prize winner in chemistry, cited 3 major reasons: 1. General companionship. At an Elderhostel you're put together with others that are still vitally active in what's going on in the world and interested in learning more things. 2. The nature of the programs. Specifically, the educational component. 3. Value and style. The programs are not as expensive as regular tour or travel agency programs. I can think of nothing worse than being stuck on a fancy cruise ship having dinners at the captain's table!

What can you learn at Elderhostel? Name a subject that interests you or about which you would like to learn more. Anything from aardvark to zyzzyva. With thousands of Elderhostels accessible and innumerable courses, the odds are high you will find what you want. To apply, the first step is to get your name added to the mailing list to receive periodic catalogs broken down alphabetically by state and specifying course offerings, price, and information regarding accommodations and the area. You can do this by mail to Boston, or by accessing Elderhostel's web address, www.elderhostel.org. Once your selection is made, you can use the application form contained in the catalog, or apply directly on the web. Catalogs also contain a Q and A section that deals with questions most frequently asked if special needs are involved.

How popular are Elderhostel programs? I met a 73-year-old woman who, over a ten-year period has signed up for 63 programs throughout the U.S. and abroad. I was told about a couple who attended the same Elderhostel 11 times (Peabody Institute of Johns Hopkins University in Baltimore, with a heavy focus on music) partly because they are music lovers and partly because it's within walking distance of their son's home.

Almost everyone knows someone who has attended one or more Elderhostels. In selecting a program ideally suited to your particular needs and tastes, your best bet is by means of personal recommendation from an a friend or acquaintance who has been there and can clue you in on the details of course content, food, lodging, and extracurricular activities.

Elderhostel is just one slice of the educational rekindlement pie for 50+ people who believe with Henry Ford that acquired knowledge is indeed a key to the fountain of youth. The prognosis is promising. Here, indicative of a growing national trend, is an excerpt from the State of Utah's Code Section 53B-9-101:

Legislative findings on higher education for senior citizens – Legislative intent – Quarterly registration fee. (1) The Legislature finds that substantial benefits would accrue to the state, as well as those directly involved, through making higher education more accessible to senior citizens who generally find themselves with more time for learning but less funds for such purposes.

(2) It is intended that an institution of higher education allow Utah residents who have reached 62 years of age to enroll at the institution, in classes for which they may be qualified, on the basis of surplus space in regularly scheduled classes in accordance with this chapter and implementing rules. These persons are exempt from tuition and other charges, except for a quarterly registration fee established by the board.

Educational options for seniors are plentiful nationwide, some free, others at modest cost. Some are state-supported, others offered by colleges and religious organizations. What follows is a small sampling. Many others can be tracked down on the Internet. Check it out.

Senior Summer School

Senior Summer School offers two and 4 week sessions taught by university professors, graduate students, teachers, and experts in various fields. As is the case with Elderhostel, focus is on "The Education Vacation." Recreational and athletic activities are available and interaction with other students is encouraged. Senior Summer School Vacations are available at the following locations: Madison, Wisconsin; Morgantown, West Virginia; San Diego, Santa Barbara, and Los Angeles, California; and Sackville, N.B., Canada. For detailed information call 1-800-847-2466, or check it out on the Internet at www.seniorsummerschool.com

City and State Programs

Several states and cities nationwide provide learning opportunities for older people. As an example, if you are 50 or older, Middletown, Ohio offers access to classes on computer technology and the Internet "to enhance their seniors' lives and enable them to share their knowledge and wisdom."

Senior Centers

Hundreds of centers throughout the U.S. arrange educational programs for seniors at local facilities or in-house. Courses are either low cost, pay what you can afford, or free.

Kislak Adult Center (Judaic-focused)

Kislak's Lifetime Learning programs feature summer lectures by renowned scholars and expert speakers in their particular field of study, Week-long sessions extend from June through September. Somewhat similar to Elderhostel programs, fees ranging from the $400s include meals, lodging with private bath, and recreational activities. (1-800-776-5657, Ext. 119).

Educational Institutions

Many colleges and universities offer learning opportunities of one form or another for older people, in most cases at a discounted rate. Typical examples:

Oklahoma University provides lecture classes at a $5 fee at its Norman campus. "Mornings with the Professor" feature volunteer lecturers, followed by a question and answer period.

University of Minnesota charges $6 a credit for courses held at its Twin Cities Campus. (That's Minneapolis/St. Paul for aliens).

Senior College Sallynoggin offers Microsoft-certified courses on the Internet and other subjects.

University of Nevada, Las Vegas has been a resource for

Continuing Education for Nevada residents 62 and older since the 1970's. Enrollees are invited to attend the Fall and Spring semester credit classes without paying credit or tuition fees. Summer credit courses are available at half price. Other classes and seminars have been designed with Senior Citizen needs in mind.

Discussion Groups on the Internet

So many different groups eager for your participation are at hand. Finding one or more specially suited to your needs should be no problem at all.

Interested in this exciting rekindlement option? Your course of action is clear. Get to work and start tracking them down.

Status quo...or status go?

Are you planning to spend the next decade or two at your current location? Or is relocating a viable option? Or perhaps you're not sure. Whatever the answer, these questions call for some of the hardest consideration and planning you will ever engage in.

Hard consideration about what? Good question. The goal in choosing where to live when you quit your job, are downsized, or sell your business, is to first decide *how* you want to live and what you most want out of life. This resolved, the next question to answer is: *Where can you best fulfill these desires and needs* – in terms of climate, community, facilities, and whatever else is involved? For example, if you're a boating enthusiast, temperate climate might be a priority. If time with the kids is essential, you might choose to relocate within reasonable commuting distance. If a new career is in the offing, it might make sense to move to an area where career opportunities abound. In response to financial considerations you would want an area where apartments or homes are affordable. If continuous learning is part of your plan, you will need a community where educational opportunities are at hand. And so on down the line.

The good news, as President Jimmy Carter said, is that the best

176

thing about winding up the time-committed work phase of your life is the freedom you have to opt for the choices that most closely satisfy your personal desires and needs. No one is better qualified than you to decide what these options might be. But a small taste of some of the most widely popular locations may help.

The Condo community alernative

Wynmoor Village, Coconut Creek, Florida

Wynmoor has more than 9,000 residents 55 years of age or over. Many are retired, actively or otherwise. A substantial number are re-**FIRED**. Some, employed part time, classify themselves as semiretired. A respectable contingent are "snow birds" who spend the winter months in Wynmoor, the summer months in cooler climes. "The best of both possible worlds," as they say. Some developments, like Wynmoor, feature apartments, some homes, some both homes and apartments.

Why do so many people in their 50's, 60's and 70's flock to condo communities like Wynmoor, or South Florida clones like Kings Point and Century Village? Well, for one thing, people need people. For another, the price is right. In Wynmoor a luxury two-bedroom, two-bath apartment runs about $110,000. A one-bedroom unit in the older section can be had for as little as $35,000.

But without question, the main drawing card for adult communities like this boils down to the services, facilities, activities, cultural, group and entertainment opportunities. Whatever your lifestyle preference, Wynmoor is likely to accommodate it, from its meticulously maintained 18-hole golf course and well kept tennis courts to its spacious theatre, grand ballroom, and a host of special purpose meeting, lecture, and card rooms. What follows is a sampling of what Wynmoor (and similar communities) have to offer:

- Gated community, security patrols.
- Health department with emergency button access.
- Security department with emergency button access.

- Free transportation to supermarkets and shopping centers.
- Broadway level shows with known artists at moderate cost.
- Late run movies ($1).
- Low cost dances with live music.
- Pop and classical concerts.
- Wynmoor's own performing orchestra.
- Contract (ACBL-certified) bridge club, and card rooms.
- Computer club and learning center.
- More cultural events than space allows to detail.
- More social clubs than space allows to detail.
- Palmetto Players – discount theatre group.
- Baseball, volley ball, shuffleboard, boccie, etc.
- Fully equipped fitness center.
- Several heated swimming pools.
- Closed circuit TV – Wynmoor's own station.

True, there's a downside. Though the terrain is beautifully land-scaped and maintained, the repetitive row after row sameness of the two and four story buildings offends some peoples' aesthetic sensibil-ities. Small price, most residents feel for all you get at low cost. Another complaint deals with the aging process. As developments age, so do their inhabitants. Many 50 and 60-olds don't want to live in a community populated by 70 and 80-year olds. Newer commu-nities attract younger people. So check it out if grandpa bothers you.

Gleneagles, Delray Beach, Florida

Gleneagles is an upscale community for the somewhat better heeled. As is the case with Wynmoor, whatever your lifestyle need and preference – cultural, educational, recreational, health and secu-rity, etc. – you are almost certain to find it here. A gated develop-ment, the resident population is roughly 2,000. Homes run from $160,000 to $360,000, apartments from $80,000 to $150,000.

An active community, Gleneagles features two golf courses and

21 Har-Tru tennis courts, plus a well equipped fitness center with three attendants. "The beauty part of Gleneagles," Micky Mazor, a totally re-**FIRED** resident, told me, "is that no one tries to outdo the other from the standpoint of material possessions." The community is also involved in a variety of charitable and pro bono activities. "It's a great life," Mazor adds, "a helluva lot better than some city streets where you're afraid to go out at night."

Wynmoor and Gleneagles clones nationwide are too numerous to document here. They range from low to high price – golf communities, beachside and mountain communities, mobile home communities, pricey dress-up country club communities, communities designed for every taste and life preference imaginable. If the concept appeals to you, check it out on the Internet.

Talk about freedom! Plan and choose wisely and active rekindlement – or lazy easy living if you prefer –can be yours for the taking. You can do what you want, when you want, where you want. In a nutshell, you got it made!

ISBN 141201144-2